# BEST of VEGAN

## 100 Recipes That Celebrate Comfort, Culture, and Community

### Kim-Julie Hansen

HARPER
DESIGN

An Imprint of HarperCollinsPublishers

**BEST OF VEGAN**

All photographs by Kim-Julie Hansen, except:
Marissa Wong (pages 32, 88, 195)
WoongHeng Chia (pages 50–51)
Seiran Sinjari (pages 111, 114)
Katharina Arrigoni (pages 174, 179)
Bronwyn Fraser (page 191)

Best of Vegan logo design by John Hansen

First published in 2022 by
Harper Design
*An Imprint* of HarperCollins*Publishers*
195 Broadway
New York, NY 10007
Tel. (212) 207-7000
Fax: (855) 746-6023

harperdesign@harpercollins.com
*www.hc.com*

Design by Laura Palese

Distributed throughout the world by
HarperCollins*Publishers*
195 Broadway
New York, NY 10007

ISBN 978-0-06-323051-4
Library of Congress Control Number: 2022938678

Printed in Thailand
First Printing, 2022

Dedicated to the
*Best of Vegan* readers,
contributors, featured
bloggers, and team
members, who have
made this community
what it is.

# PART 4 — BEST OF VEGAN BAKING 158

# PART 5 — BEST OF VEGAN BASICS 202

# INTRODUCTION

## Welcome to the *Best of Vegan* cookbook.

This book is the result of years of collaboration, stories told, meals shared, trial and error, and so much more. Before you continue reading, I want you to know that you don't need to be vegan to enjoy these recipes. My goal is not to convince or persuade you of anything. I'm here to share what will (hopefully) become some of your new favorite recipes and to offer you a glimpse into the marvelously versatile world that is vegan cuisine.

If this book ends up motivating you to adopt a more plant-based lifestyle, great. If it makes you want to start eating one vegan meal a day, a week, a month, or even a year, amazing. If it inspires you to think about where our food comes from and the ways in which the dishes we cook are linked to our memories and culture, wonderful. And if all it does is just give you a few new meal ideas, that is fantastic too. Just know that it is for everyone, no matter where you currently are in your journey.

On the following pages, I'll be sharing a bit more about Best of Vegan, the platform that inspired this book; veganism and how it relates to culture and identity; and how to use this book to ensure you get the most out of it.

## About Best of Vegan

Best of Vegan is a digital culinary and lifestyle publication with a global reach of over two million people. It all started with an Instagram account (@bestofvegan) that I launched in early 2014, and it has since been dedicated to showcasing recipes from chefs, bloggers, and enthusiastic home cooks, as well as restaurant reviews, tutorials, and articles covering culture, culinary topics, and all things food and veganism. I created the account with one simple desire in mind: to show people how delicious vegan food can really be. The title of this book is an extension of the online platform, and the term *best* refers to the collective talent that has inspired, encouraged, and fueled this continuously growing global community. In a world where many still confuse veganism with a fad diet or a boring way to eat, this book will give you a bird's-eye view of everything that vegan food can be and show you how to veganize your favorite style of eating, whether that's comfort food, cultural food, healthy(ish) food, sweet food, or all of the above.

## Veganism, Food, Identity, and Culture

Veganism is a lifestyle that excludes all animal products (as far as possible), including those found in food, cosmetics, clothes, and other products, such as furniture and household items. It also excludes products tested on animals and activities involving animals used for entertainment (like the zoo, circus, or aquarium). While some choose to stop eating meat for environmental or health reasons, veganism is, by definition, an ethical choice. Anyone who decides to limit their intake of animal products for nonethical reasons is referred to as plant-based. Though the impact may be quite similar, making this distinction might help explain why some vegans embrace any food that is vegan, including desserts, burgers, pasta, and pies, while others choose a more health-oriented diet. Veganism is not synonymous with a healthy diet, but it certainly can include a health-conscious mindset if desired; there isn't just *one* way to eat vegan.

"Being vegetarian here also means that we do not consume dairy and egg products, because they are products of the meat industry."
—THICH NHAT HANH

"Food is not rational. Food is culture, habit, craving, and identity."
—JONATHAN SAFRAN FOER

The term *vegan* was coined in the United Kingdom by Donald Watson in the 1940s to provide a simpler term for a person who until then had been referred to as a nondairy vegetarian who also excludes eggs (or, sometimes, a strict vegetarian). Watson also founded the UK Vegan Society, an organization that still provides information on and resources for a vegan lifestyle.

While the name is relatively recent, the concept of reducing animal products and living a predominantly plant-based lifestyle is not a new one. Throughout history, there have been many famous proponents of a lifestyle that minimizes the use of animal products, including Pythagoras, Mary Shelley, and Franz Kafka. They made their opinions heard, but since there was no clear distinction between vegetarians who ate some animal products, such as eggs and cheese, and those who did not, it is difficult to pinpoint exactly when and where the movement originated.

It is, however, important to note that veganism didn't just appear out of thin air in the 1940s; its roots are far reaching and connected to cultures around the world. In many places, like the Japanese islands of Okinawa, and regions across China, India, and the African continent, people have relied on plants like potatoes, corn, cassava, and rice as their dietary staples, with meat and other animal products either being rare or seen as supplemental rather than essential. With plants playing such an important role, quite a lot of beloved cultural foods, especially side dishes, are easy to veganize. Yet we're so used to thinking in a binary way that we don't realize that vegan food isn't so different from nonvegan food, especially if we consider that meat, fish, and other animal products get their depth of flavor from seasonings and condiments, which are usually plant-based. However, there's a vital aspect of food that makes it much trickier to change one's dietary habits than to, say, switch from plastic utensils to reusable ones or to take public transport and shorter showers. Food is intrinsically linked to our identity and culture.

One of the reasons veganism is such a controversial topic is that restricting the food we eat can seem akin to removing part of our identity. I grew up amid several different cultures, and food was the centerpiece of family gatherings and other social traditions. I am Belgian, Scottish, and Congolese on my mother's side and Scandinavian, Frisian, and Irish on my father's side. I have lived and worked in diverse countries, including the United States, Germany, Italy, New Zealand, France, Egypt, and Belgium. When I think of waffles, I think of rainy afternoons spent walking through the cobblestoned streets of Brussels's historic city center, holding a paper-wrapped hot waffle with powdered sugar in one hand and chocolate milk in the other. Every afternoon at 3:00 p.m., I'm reminded of the German tradition of *Kaffee und Kuchen*, which simply translates to "coffee and cake." It's the only German tradition my mother happily embraced after moving to Berlin in her midtwenties. Occasionally, we would go to a Konditorei, pick out our favorite cake slices, and then serve them to our guests with hot coffee and tea, a tradition I'd later continue (and slightly modernize) at coffee shops with friends. For Christmas Day each year, my Belgian family would prepare ham and boudins, a type of sausage often eaten on special occasions. I learned all about *moambé*, a Congolese palm butter and chicken dish, from my great-uncle Johnnie, who'd often stop by my grandmother's house to make it. He'd tell me stories of his mother—my great-grandmother—cooking it for him as a child in the 1930s and how the taste and smell would still transport him right back to Bwendaki, his hometown near Budjala in northern Congo.

All these memories are a part of who I am and something I want to hold on to, not distance myself from. Every time I meet someone from another culture, I learn about *their* memories and the foods *they* grew up loving. Whether it's my friend Yamina teaching me how to make her favorite Moroccan dish, Tajine Kefta (a meatball dish served with potatoes and a tomato-based spicy sauce), or my friend Ko telling me about eating *champuru* (a type of stir-fry) on Okinawa as a child, we all have memories that are linked to food.

It seems natural that the mere idea of removing the foods we love from our lives, whether they're from our own culture(s) or those we've learned to appreciate, would be threatening and trigger a lot of strong emotions. When I went vegan more than ten years ago, my very first thought was, "Oh no, I'll never be able to enjoy lattes and sushi again." I, of course, didn't realize that almost everything can be made vegan with just a little creativity and the right ingredients. What started as a huge perceived personal sacrifice became a journey of discovery that, to this day, remains both fascinating and exciting. Many modern vegan products have a flavor profile almost identical to that of their animal-derived counterparts. And while that's undoubtedly remarkable, as with anything in life, there are those who criticize and reject this trend. But I believe that these products make it much easier for people to embrace vegan meals.

To be honest, I don't think I would have stuck with veganism for as long as I have if it weren't for vegan cheese, meats, milk, and even eggs. Luckily, though, there are many dishes that don't require veganized animal products, so if you're not a fan, no need to worry. There are plenty of other options to choose from!

> "I think there needs to be a general consciousness raising among consumers. So many consumers aren't aware of the backstory. They see the end product in the supermarket but don't know all the steps that it took to get it there, who helped to get the food there."
> —BRYANT TERRY

Beyond our emotional and cultural relationships with food, our daily choices and habits have very real consequences. Before going vegan, I hardly ever thought about where (and whom) my food came from. I just took it for granted that everything I wanted and needed was readily available at my local supermarket. I was also not an animal lover and never thought it strange that we treat our pets so differently from the animals we raise for food.

It wasn't until I was in college and accidentally took a vegetarian to a steakhouse that I started digging deeper. We had intended to go to an Italian restaurant, but when I saw that it was closed, I made the executive decision to switch restaurants and made a reservation at a steakhouse instead, not realizing that a member of our group was vegetarian. He did his best to conceal his disappointment, but something about seeing him eating his little side salad surrounded by a dozen people devouring steaks and ribs set off

a personal quest in me. I began by asking him a ton of questions about protein, his favorite meals, vitamin deficiencies, if he ever missed meat, and so on. This quest later led me to read the books *Eating Animals* by Jonathan Safran Foer and *Slaughterhouse* by Gail Eisnitz. Right before reading *Eating Animals*, I had started working on a paper called "Why Vegetarianism Isn't Necessary" for one of my college classes (the steakhouse incident had impacted me enough to start asking questions, but not enough to fully convince me yet). As I finished reading the last page of Foer's book, I vowed to no longer eat meat and changed the title of my essay to "Why Eating Meat Should Be Illegal." That's how much what I'd just learned had shocked me.

But it was *Slaughterhouse* that made me go fully vegan overnight. I won't detail here what the book unveiled, but if you've ever been curious about what conditions in factory farms and slaughterhouses are really like and whether the cruel cases we occasionally hear about on the news are exceptions, I'd highly recommend reading both of these books (I've included a list of book and documentary recommendations in the Resources section, page 216).

I don't think that anything I say or do could convince you to change the way you eat unless it's something you want to do, but I would encourage everyone to at least do enough research to make an informed decision. What it ultimately boils down to for me is that if we don't need animal products to thrive or even to survive, then looking for alternatives whenever possible and practicable is the compassionate thing to do.

For a serving of meat to land on our plates, an animal must be bred, raised, and fed—often in the most inhumane of conditions—then slaughtered while still very young, packaged, transported, bought, seasoned, and cooked. Somewhere along that chain, we lose all the connection and empathy we would have had, had we met the animal while it was still alive. The system relies on our disconnection to continue to capitalize. But if we don't need animal products to be healthy, if we're wasting more resources than we are creating (for instance, it takes more food to raise animals for food than those animals end up producing), and if the environmental impact of this production significantly contributes to greenhouse gas emissions and global warming, then there comes a point when we seriously need to question and reevaluate our practices. I don't think it's fair to transfer this responsibility to the consumer alone, but by asking ourselves these important questions, we have an opportunity to contribute to a broader conversation and thus demand change on a systemic and legislative level. It is also important to remember that not everyone has access to the same information and resources, and therefore the conversation about animal agriculture, animal rights, and the food industry at large must also address the inequalities that impact us all differently. Rather than judge those who do not have access to the same resources, it might be wiser and more compassionate to work on solutions to increase accessibility and equal opportunities for all.

## A Collaborative Cookbook

Community is the cornerstone of this book. Many of the recipes you'll see here are collaborations with friends and family, colleagues, chefs, restaurant owners, and other people whose work I've admired for years. From its inception, the Best of Vegan platform has been community based, and it simply would not exist without the help, contributions, and feedback from so many people, including thousands of featured bloggers and chefs and millions of readers around the

world. The recipes in this book were developed in Belgium, Japan, the United Kingdom, Panama, Switzerland, New Zealand, Brazil, the United States, the Netherlands, and many other places. They were tested by Best of Vegan readers in countries including Jamaica, Germany, Australia, Canada, Austria, and the United States, and then photographed in Belgium, Hawaii, Switzerland, Sweden, and Canada.

Similarly, food itself is very much community based. Whether it's cooking with friends and family, enjoying new dishes at a restaurant, or reading about the stories behind our favorite recipes, there's always an element of togetherness that I hope shines through these pages as well. Food has the power to transcend time and space through flavors, scents, and textures, and it can therefore bring us closer together in so many ways. I never got to meet my great-grandmother Lusiyah, but listening to my great-uncle tell me stories about her while cooking her favorite meals and then tasting the same dishes she used to eat make me feel like I am getting to know her at least a little bit.

## How to Use This Book

The five parts of this book are meant to be used in connection with each other, and the lines between some of the categories are intentionally blurred. The first part, for instance, is dedicated to comfort food, but that doesn't mean that the recipes in the

"Eating is so intimate. It's very sensual. When you invite someone to sit at your table and you want to cook for them, you're inviting a person into your life."
—MAYA ANGELOU

other chapters aren't also comforting. The second part includes recipes that celebrate cultures and our personal connections to them. You'll also find a few more cultural recipes throughout the other chapters, like the tiramisu in the dessert section. The third part, "Wholesome," includes plant-centric and healthy-ish recipes, meaning they're not too strict about the "healthy" label and they celebrate a balanced lifestyle. The fourth part includes desserts, both baked and unbaked. The final part, "Best of Vegan Basics," contains recipes for staple foods like vegan whipped cream, sour cream, nut milks, and condiments.

Labels like "high protein," "gluten-free," "tree nut-free," and "lazy vegan" are meant to help you easily decide which recipe to try next. While the first three are self-explanatory, "lazy vegan" refers to recipes that either require minimal prep work and/or cleanup, or are very easy and quick to make.

This book provides both metric and imperial measurements to make it more accessible for all cooks.

## Playlist (Food and Music)

Does a specific smell or taste ever transport you right back to your childhood? What about a sound or a song? Our senses have the power to not only transport us back in time, but also allow us to travel from within our kitchens and dinner tables. The hours of conversations that accompanied the recipe collaborations in this book brought back many memories and emotions for everyone involved. To convey that sentiment, I decided to include a playlist to go with it. There are one or more songs for each recipe that you can listen to while you're cooking and/or eating. You'll also find an extended playlist for each recipe on the book's website mentioned below. The list was cocurated by many of the people featured

 **Gluten-free**
This recipe naturally contains no gluten.

 **Gluten-free option**
This recipe provides suggestions for gluten-free alternatives

 **Tree nut-free**
This recipe excludes nuts that grow on trees (one of the most common allergens) like cashews, hazelnuts, almonds, and walnuts.

 **Lazy Vegan**
This recipe either requires minimal prep work and/or cleanup, or is quick and easy to make.

**High Protein**
This recipe is high in plant protein derived from beans, nuts, seeds, and/or other protein sources.

> **"Food and music are the international language."**
> —DANIEL HAIMONA

throughout the chapters, but also by close friends who are music connoisseurs. It offers a mix of songs that are either linked to the recipes themselves (and the cultures they're from) or are simply songs we thought you would enjoy listening to while cooking.

## Bonus Content

There were far more ideas for this book than the number of pages available. It has therefore become a book with this bonus online content:

- Vegan Meal-Prep Guide
- Vegan on a Budget
- Vegan Guide to Protein
- 7-Day Sample Meal Plan and Grocery Shopping List

To receive these guides, simply email a copy of your receipt or forward your order confirmation to cookbook@bestofvegan.com. You'll also find additional content at bestofvegan.com/mycookbook (scan the QR code to go directly to this page), as well

as thousands of recipes at bestofvegan.com. If you'd like to receive recipes directly in your inbox, you can sign up at bestofvegan.com/newsletter.

**THE RECIPES:**

# Why Recreate Vegan Versions of Nonvegan Dishes? (And Why Not Just Call Them Something Else?)

Since this book includes a few recipes that either use faux meats (and other vegan alternatives to animal products) or seek to recreate them in other ways, I thought it was important to address this topic briefly to hopefully avoid any confusion or unanswered questions. According to some critics, vegan foods should not mimic animal products, nor should the names of animal-based foods (cheese, butter, meat, etc.) be used in describing plant-based alternatives. "Why do vegans keep trying to recreate animal products even though they no longer want to eat them?" That's a question I see quite often when we share these kinds of recipes on Best of Vegan. It's because veganism, at its core, has nothing to do with not wanting to eat animal products and everything to do with not wanting to harm animals. Many of us grew up eating and loving animal products and made the switch only for ethical reasons. That doesn't erase a lifetime of memories associated with eating meat, fish, eggs, and dairy. Recreating plant-based versions and calling them "vegan tuna," "vegan steak," and so on allows us to still enjoy versions of these foods and to easily identify them. Someone who misses tuna isn't going to search for "marinated and baked watermelon cubes." Adding *vegan* further clarifies that it's not, in fact, fish, thereby avoiding any confusion.

Veganism is a rapidly growing movement, and the importance of catering to all preferences and taste buds can't and shouldn't be underestimated. Veganizing meals is essential in helping plant-based options become more mainstream. Culinary traditions across the globe have perfected the art of seasoning and cooking meat dishes, making them an intrinsic part of our cultural identities. By offering alternatives that mimic animal products in taste, texture, and even appearance, chefs and companies have recognized an opportunity to minimize any perceived sacrifice by helping consumers enjoy and recreate their favorite dishes. In addition, more and more people who aren't yet ready to go fully vegan are at least becoming open to including more plant-based meals for environmental and/or health reasons. These products are therefore targeted at both vegans and nonvegans, further explaining the need for and importance of alternatives that resemble animal products so closely.

I find it very interesting that we've actually perfected the art of making animals *not* look and taste like animals (I don't know about you, but growing up, my fish sticks looked nothing like fish and my chicken nuggets bore no resemblance to live chickens). That's why I believe that describing vegan products using terms associated with nonvegan foods isn't as problematic as some make it out to be. Overall, I find it to be more helpful than not.

> "[A]nd peanut butter isn't butter, quince cheese isn't cheese, cream of coconut isn't cream . . . try as dairy farmers might, history and the nature of language development will decide."
> —STEPHEN FRY

For clarity, I've chosen a middle ground, using "buffalo cauliflower bites" instead of "wings," for example, but also "vegan chicken" and 'fish' fillets. Just know that every ingredient listed in this book is vegan.

## Measurements

The measurements included are both imperial and metric. Whenever the conversion resulted in uneven or otherwise complicated measurements, I've rounded up or down as long as it had no impact on the outcome of the recipe.

In the United States, cans (of beans, for example) are most commonly referred to by their total weight, including any brine or other liquid, not the net weight as in other parts of the world. To keep it consistent, I've used the total weight for both ounces and grams throughout the book, so if you see a 400-gram can of beans, that includes both the weight of the actual beans (usually about 250 grams) and the weight of the liquid included with the beans.

Whenever flour is listed, it is meant to be spooned into the cup(s), not packed. The grams listed reflect this, so if you're ever unsure, you can double-check by using a kitchen scale. This can make a big difference in recipes, especially when it comes to baked goods, so please keep this in mind.

## Disclaimer

All nutritional information in this book has been reviewed by registered dietitian and author Gena Hamshaw.

# I Don't Want Salad

**HEN I WENT VEGAN,** there wasn't a single vegan restaurant in the city where I lived. During my frequent work trips, I'd find myself in remote places where, more often than not, the restaurant staff didn't even know exactly what *vegan* meant. I'd explain the same thing over and over: "It's basically vegetarian, but without eggs, milk, cheese, and honey . . ." What followed nine times out of ten was a moment of silence, a confused look, and then the epiphany—"Oh, salad!" No, no, no, no. I did not want salad. At all. I didn't go vegan because I loved vegetables, I went vegan because I no longer wanted to support animal agriculture (and even though I had always *loved* the taste of meat, eggs, and dairy).

I'd never liked salads, and going vegan didn't magically change that. So, as I looked at the sad lettuce leaves on my plate (usually paired with even sadder-looking cold tomatoes and cucumbers), I wondered how I could avoid this dilemma moving forward. I thus resorted to giving the restaurant staff specific suggestions rather than telling them what I couldn't, or rather wouldn't, eat. "Potatoes, egg-free pasta, rice, beans. Just with olive oil instead of butter and cheese, please." This worked like a charm, and my sad lunches became pasta-filled feasts.

The stereotype of vegans eating nothing but salad persists nonetheless, and I'm far from being the only one trying to refute it. Years ago, my friend Jessica, whose husband and kids were also vegan at the time, left me a distraught voice message after spending a holiday at her parents' house. She told me about how she'd had no time to eat that whole day and was really looking forward to a delicious dinner. As her father set the table, one dish after another was covered in cheese. She looked at him, visibly disappointed, to which he cheerily responded: "Don't worry, I prepared a salad for you!" Jessica blurted out her frustration to me: "Salad! Can you believe it?! Salad?! I DON'T WANT SALAD." A sentiment that undoubtedly resonates with so many comfort-food-loving vegans.

While I have since reluctantly taught myself to love certain salads (more about that in part 3), my brother, John, has not. Nor does he have any desire to ever overcome his distaste for them. On the contrary, he found the cover of my first book, *Vegan Reset*, which was filled with pictures of fresh fruits and vegetables, offensive and not inviting in the least. His exact words, I believe, were, "I mean, I guess I'll buy it 'cause you're my sister, but if you weren't, I wouldn't even have picked it up." Fair enough. This part of the book is dedicated to him and everyone who feels like he does.

# BAJA-STYLE "FISH" TACOS

In collaboration with
Chef Charly Garcia, Charly's
Vegan Tacos

Yield: 6 tacos

*Prep time: 30 minutes*
*Cook time: 15 minutes*
*Total time: 45 minutes*

The best tacos I've ever had were from Charly's Vegan Tacos in Tulúm, a town on the coastline of Mexico's Yucatán Peninsula. Their tacos, which are now also served at their Miami location, are packed with flavor thanks to Chef Charly's years spent modifying his grandmother's secret recipes in order to recreate the homemade taste of his favorite, authentic Mexican food. His motto? "Designed for meat lovers, made for vegans." Instead of fish, this recipe uses crispy fried hearts of palm, served in soft and warm corn tortillas, topped with shredded cabbage and a spicy sauce.

½ purple cabbage, julienned

2 large limes: 1 juiced, 1 cut into 6 wedges

1 teaspoon sea salt, plus more to taste

½ teaspoon ground black pepper, plus more to taste

1 small, fresh pineapple

2 bunches of fresh cilantro, stems removed

1½ cups (360 mL) vegan mayonnaise

½ cup (100 g) chipotles in adobo sauce (from a 7-ounce/200 g can)

1 quart (1 L) neutral high-heat vegetable oil, such as sunflower seed or avocado oil

3 nori sheets

6 hearts of palm (from a can or jar)

1 cup (125 g) all-purpose flour (gluten-free if desired)

1 cup (240 mL) beer, alcohol-free if desired (for a gluten-free alternative to beer, use club soda instead)

1 teaspoon sea salt

½ teaspoon ground black pepper

1 teaspoon dried oregano

1 teaspoon garlic powder

1 teaspoon onion powder

½ cup (60 g) cornstarch

*TO SERVE*
6 soft corn tortillas

1. **To make the slaw:** Mix the purple cabbage with the juice of 1 lime. Add salt and pepper to taste. Set aside. Pare and dice the pineapple, roughly chop the cilantro, and set aside separately.

2. **To make the chipotle mayo:** Combine the vegan mayo and chipotles in adobo sauce in a blender or food processor and blend until smooth.

3. **To make the "fish":** In a large pot, heat the oil until it reaches 340°F (170°C).

4. Place the nori sheets in a food processor or blender and pulse until you have a powder.

5. Rinse and dry the palm hearts and cut in half lengthwise. Dust generously with the nori powder.

6. Combine the flour, beer, salt, pepper, oregano, garlic powder, and onion powder in a bowl and mix until smooth.

7. Pour the cornstarch into a separate bowl.

8. Dip each palm heart in the cornstarch, then in the beer batter, coating evenly, and set aside on a plate until all are coated.

9. Carefully place each battered palm heart in the hot oil using tongs and fry until golden brown, about 4 to 5 minutes, turning them halfway through to make sure they're fried evenly. Adjust the heat as needed to maintain the temperature.

10. Warm the tortillas in a hot dry skillet or the oven and place 2 palm heart "fish" pieces on each tortilla. Top with the slaw, pineapple, cilantro, and chipotle mayo. Serve with a lime wedge on the side.

"Con Tus Besos" by Eslabon Armado

I Don't Want Salad

**APPETIZERS & SIDES**

18

# BEER-BATTER-FRIED
# OYSTER MUSHROOMS

Yield: 4 servings

(as an appetizer or side dish)

*Prep time: 15 to 20 minutes*
*Cook time: 15 minutes*
*Total time: 30 to 35 minutes*

Oyster mushrooms are among the most versatile mushrooms that exist. Like tofu, you can season, marinate, shred, chop, sauté, boil, or bake them to achieve your desired flavor profile and texture, making them an ideal centerpiece of many savory dishes. This is one of my favorite ways to enjoy them.

*FOR THE BATTER*

1 cup (125 g) all-purpose flour

1 tablespoon chickpea flour (or more all-purpose flour)

¼ teaspoon baking soda

1⅓ cups (320 mL) cold beer, alcohol-free if desired

1½ teaspoons sea salt

1½ teaspoons garlic powder

1½ teaspoons onion powder

1 teaspoon smoked paprika

1 pinch of ground coriander

1 teaspoon Old Bay seasoning or ½ shredded nori sheet (optional; see Note)

*FOR THE MUSHROOMS*

18 ounces (500 g) king oyster or oyster mushrooms

¼ cup (30 g) cornstarch (optional)

1 quart (1L) neutral high-heat vegetable oil

*TO SERVE*

Juice of ½ lemon (1 tablespoon)

Dip/sauce of your choice (vegan tartar sauce, BBQ sauce, etc.)

Fresh dill (optional)

**1. Prepare the batter:** Add all the batter ingredients to a bowl and mix using a whisk, being careful not to overmix!

**2. Prepare the oyster mushrooms:** If you have king oyster mushrooms (with thick, long stems), slice the stems lengthwise. If you have regular oyster mushrooms (the caps), leave them whole (separate them only if several caps are connected). If using the cornstarch, place the mushrooms in a ziplock bag or reusable container. Add the cornstarch to the mushrooms and shake until they are evenly coated with the starch. (This step is optional, but I find that the batter sticks to the mushrooms a bit better if you add cornstarch first.)

**3.** Add the mushrooms to the bowl with the batter, making sure they're all submerged and coated.

**4.** Heat the oil in a large pot until it reaches about 340°F (170°C). The oil needs to be at least ½ to 1 inch (1.25 to 2.5 cm) high.

**5.** Once the oil reaches the desired temperature, add the mushrooms and fry for 2 to 2½ minutes on each side, until golden brown.

**6.** Using tongs or a slotted spoon, remove the mushrooms and place them on a kitchen towel or in a strainer to drain excess oil.

**7.** Pat the mushrooms dry, sprinkle with the lemon juice, and serve with fresh dill and with your favorite dip or sauce, such as a vegan tartar sauce (see page 35).

## NOTE

*Using either the Old Bay seasoning or the nori sheet will give the mushrooms a flavor profile that is often associated with seafood dishes. If you're using nori or choose to omit this step, be sure to add a little more salt to taste.*

♫ "As" by Stevie Wonder

# BUFFALO CAULIFLOWER BITES

**Yield: 2 large or 4 small servings**

*Prep time: 20 minutes*
*Cook time: 35 minutes*
*Total time: 55 minutes*

These buffalo cauliflower bites are popular among both meat eaters and vegans. They're crispy and tender, just spicy enough (with a touch of sweetness), and the perfect snack or appetizer to enjoy on game day, at parties, or just for a cozy night in. You can serve them with your favorite dips or fresh veggies, or turn them into a meal with some rice or a soup.

♪ "Anything" by SWV, feat. Wu-Tang Clan

GFO

TNF

## FOR THE CAULIFLOWER

- 1¼ cups (160 g) all-purpose flour, gluten-free if desired
- 2 teaspoons garlic powder
- 1 teaspoon onion powder
- 1 teaspoon paprika
- ½ teaspoon ground black pepper
- 1 teaspoon sea salt
- 1½ cups (360 mL) unsweetened soy or oat milk
- 1 large cauliflower head, cut into florets
- 2 cups (120 g) panko bread crumbs, gluten-free if desired

## FOR THE BUFFALO SAUCE

- ¼ to ½ cup (60 to 120 mL) hot sauce (see Note)
- ¼ cup (60 mL) soy sauce or gluten-free tamari
- ¼ cup (60 mL) maple syrup
- 2 tablespoons cornstarch
- ¼ cup (60 mL) apple cider vinegar
- ¼ cup (60 mL) water
- ½ cup (114 g) vegan butter

## TO SERVE

- Vegan sour cream
- Veggies of choice (like carrot and celery sticks)
- BBQ sauce or any other dips/sauces of your choice

1. Preheat the oven to 400°F (200°C), using the fan or convection oven setting (if you don't have this setting, simply use your oven's regular setting, but increase the heat to 425°F/220°C). Line a large baking tray with parchment paper.

2. **Prepare the cauliflower:** In a large bowl, combine the flour, garlic powder, onion powder, paprika, pepper, and salt. Slowly pour in the milk, mixing it in with a whisk or fork until you get a smooth, lump-free consistency.

3. Add all the cauliflower florets to the bowl and toss until well coated.

4. Gently shake off excess batter, then dip the florets one by one into a bowl filled with the breadcrumbs. Next, place them on the baking tray using your hands, a fork, or tongs. Make sure you leave a little space between the florets.

5. Bake for 35 minutes, flipping them halfway through, until crispy.

6. **Prepare the buffalo sauce:** While the florets are baking, in a small bowl whisk all the sauce ingredients except the vegan butter. Melt the vegan butter in a small pot over medium heat. Once melted, add the other ingredients to the butter and whisk until the sauce thickens (this takes only 1 to 2 minutes), then remove from the heat and set aside.

7. Once the florets are baked, take them out of the oven and dip them in the buffalo sauce, either one by one or all at once.

8. Serve warm with vegan sour cream, cut veggies, and the dipping sauces of your choice.

## NOTES

• If you'd like your bites to be milder, use only ¼ cup (60 mL of hot sauce). If you're making these for children, I'd recommend replacing the buffalo sauce with ketchup or BBQ sauce.

• If you have any buffalo sauce leftover, you can mix it into vegan mayonnaise for a homemade spicy mayo.

# CHEESY ARTICHOKE & BROCCOLI DIP

Yield: 6 to 8 servings

Prep time: 10 to 15 minutes
Cook time: 35 minutes
Total time: 45 to 50 minutes

This one's a definite crowd pleaser! It's inspired by my grandmother Maggie's famous baked artichoke dip, which she makes anytime there's a birthday or other celebration because it's so easy to prepare, and everyone loves it.

1 tablespoon olive oil

6 garlic cloves, minced

1 small onion, finely chopped

2 cups (150 g) chopped fresh broccoli florets

1 3.5-ounce (100 g) bag spinach or baby spinach

1½ cups (150 g) shredded vegan mozzarella

¼ cup (60 mL) vegan mayonnaise

½ cup (120 mL) vegan sour cream or vegan cream cheese

3 tablespoons grated vegan parmesan

3 tablespoons nutritional yeast

1 tablespoon cornstarch

½ teaspoon sea salt, or to taste

¼ teaspoon ground black pepper

1 14-ounce (400 g) can artichoke hearts, drained and pressed (to remove excess liquid), then chopped

**TO SERVE**
Tortilla chips or bread (like baguette or ciabatta, gluten-free if desired), for serving

**1.** Preheat the oven to 350°F (180°C).

**2.** Warm the olive oil in a large skillet. Add the garlic, onion, broccoli, and spinach, and sauté over medium heat for 8 to 10 minutes.

**3.** In a large bowl, mix all the remaining ingredients (except the tortilla chips), then fold in the sautéed veggies.

**4.** Transfer the mixture to a deep small to medium baking dish and bake for 20 minutes (or until the cheese has melted), then broil for an additional 3 to 5 minutes, until the dip is bubbling and lightly browned.

**5.** Serve with tortilla chips or bread.

 "Mon Eldorado" by Yannick Noah

GF

LV

I Don't Want Salad

**APPETIZERS & SIDES**

# CLASSIC VEGAN
# MAC 'N' CHEESE

### Yield: 2 servings

*Prep time: 5 minutes*
*Cook time: 10 minutes*
*Total time: 15 minutes*

There's nothing quite like a comforting bowl of mac 'n' cheese. If you look for plant-based mac 'n' cheese recipes online, you'll find a variety of cashew and other nut-based sauces that are all delightful (the creamy veggie pasta recipe in this book uses a similar base), but I wanted to include a recipe that requires no blender, as well as minimal preparation, time, and effort. It's the kind of recipe I make whenever I'm impatient and just want an easy, delicious meal in no time.

I Don't Want Salad

PASTA

- 6 ounces (170 g) macaroni, gluten-free if desired
- ½ teaspoon olive oil
- 2 tablespoons panko bread crumbs, gluten-free if desired
- 2 tablespoons vegan butter
- 2 tablespoons all-purpose flour, gluten-free if desired
- 1 to 1½ cups (240 to 360 mL) unsweetened plant milk
- 2 cups (200 g) shredded vegan cheese (ideally, a mix of mozzarella-, cheddar-, and gouda-style cheeses, but any type will do) or more, nut-free if desired
- 1 teaspoon garlic powder
- 1 pinch of sea salt, or to taste
- 1 pinch of ground black pepper
- ½ teaspoon smoked paprika
- 2 tablespoons chopped fresh herbs like curly parsley or chives (optional)

**1.** Cook the pasta according to the package instructions. Drain and set aside.

**2.** Meanwhile, toast the bread crumbs: Warm the olive oil in a small nonstick pan, then add the bread crumbs and toast over medium high heat until golden brown, 2 to 3 minutes (be sure to watch closely so they don't burn).

**3.** In a separate pot, melt the butter over medium to high heat. Whisk in the flour, then add the milk, continuing to whisk until smooth and thickened.

**4.** Add the cheese, garlic powder, salt, pepper, and paprika and mix, using a wooden spoon or spatula. When the cheese is almost fully melted, add the pasta. Stir again and cook for another 30 seconds, until the cheese is fully melted. Add more milk and/or butter if needed to either thin or thicken the sauce to achieve your desired consistency.

**5.** Top with the toasted bread crumbs and fresh herbs (if using).

"Check the Rhime" by A Tribe Called Quest

# RED WINE TEMPEH PECAN BOLOGNESE-STYLE PASTA

Yield: 2 servings

*Prep time: 15 minutes*
*Cook time: 15 minutes*
*Total time: 30 minutes*

This is a twist on spaghetti Bolognese, my favorite childhood recipe. The robust flavors and hearty ingredients make for a very filling and satisfying meal that is great for dinner parties or a romantic date night in. Or how about dinner for one paired with a glass of wine and a movie? You can then either freeze the leftovers or enjoy them for lunch the next day.

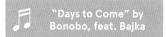

"Days to Come" by Bonobo, feat. Bajka

- 6 ounces (170 g) pasta of your choice, gluten-free if desired (see Notes)
- 1 red onion, sliced
- 4 garlic cloves, minced, or more to taste
- 1 tablespoon olive oil
- 7 to 8 ounces (200 to 225 g) tempeh (see Notes)
- ⅓ cup (35 g) roughly chopped pecans or walnuts
- 10 oil-packed sun-dried tomatoes, ideally unsalted, roughly chopped
- ¼ teaspoon sea salt, or to taste
- 1 pinch of ground black pepper
- 1 teaspoon dried oregano (see Notes), or more to taste
- 1 teaspoon dried basil, or more to taste
- ¼ cup (60 mL) red wine (or more vegetable broth)
- ¼ cup (60 mL) vegetable broth
- 2 cups (480 mL) tomato-basil sauce (see Notes)
- 2 teaspoons coconut sugar or maple syrup
- ½ cup (50 g) vegan mozzarella shreds, or as much as your heart desires (optional)

*TO SERVE*

Fresh basil (whole leaves or chopped)

Vegan parmesan (page 206; optional)

Cherry tomatoes, halved (optional)

**1.** Cook the pasta according to the package instructions (usually for 7 to 10 minutes). Drain and set aside.

**2.** While the pasta is cooking, sauté the onion and garlic in the olive oil in a medium saucepan over medium-high heat for 5 minutes.

**3.** Crumble the tempeh using a fork or your hands, then add it to the pan along with the pecans, sun-dried tomatoes, salt, pepper, oregano, and basil. Reduce the heat to medium, mix well, and cook for 5 more minutes.

**4.** Add the red wine first, then the vegetable broth, tomato sauce, and coconut sugar. Mix again, reduce the heat to medium-low, and simmer for 5 more minutes. Mix in the vegan mozzarella during the last 2 to 3 minutes, until it's melted into the sauce.

**5.** Top the pasta with the sauce, fresh basil, and vegan parmesan, if using.

## NOTES

- *To make this recipe gluten-free, use lentil or chickpea pasta.*

- *Tempeh is a protein-rich food made from fermented soybeans. Its taste can take some people a while to get used to, but this is actually the perfect recipe to get accustomed to it because the other ingredients even out its flavor, making it a lot milder.*

- *You can use 2 teaspoons Italian seasoning in place of the basil and oregano.*

- *If there's no tomato-basil sauce in your cupboard, you can use a can of tomato puree mixed with 1 tablespoon Italian seasoning and sea salt to taste.*

GFO

HP

I Don't Want Salad

PASTA

# CHIPOTLE CURRY "CHICKEN" WRAPS

**Yield: 2 large or 4 small wraps**

*Prep time: 10 minutes*
*Cook time: 10 minutes*
*Total time: 20 minutes*

If you're on the go and need an easy, protein-rich, and flavorful lunch idea, you'll love this recipe. It's easy to make and super filling. I love wraps because you can just fill them with all your favorite ingredients and then tuck them in your lunch box or eat them with some rice or hummus.

- 1 tablespoon olive oil
- 1 medium yellow or white onion, chopped
- 2 large garlic cloves, minced
- 1 red bell pepper, chopped
- 1 5.6-ounce (160 g) package vegan chicken strips, cut into ½- to 1-inch (1.25 to 2.5 cm) pieces (see Note)
- 2 teaspoons curry powder (less if you like it milder)
- 1 teaspoon chipotle powder (less if you like it milder)
- ½ teaspoon sea salt, or to taste
- ¼ teaspoon ground black pepper
- 1 tablespoon tomato paste
- 1 teaspoon coconut sugar
- ¼ cup (60 mL) water
- 2 large or 4 small whole wheat tortillas (use corn tortillas for gluten-free wraps)
- Fresh curly parsley, roughly chopped, to garnish

**1.** In a large skillet, warm the olive oil over medium heat. Once the pan is hot, add the onion, garlic, and bell pepper and sauté for 3 minutes.

**2.** Add the vegan chicken, curry powder, chipotle powder, salt, and pepper and cook for 3 more minutes.

**3.** Mix in the tomato paste, coconut sugar, and water and stir well. Let simmer over medium-low heat for 4 minutes, until the sauce is reduced slightly and the "chicken" is fully cooked.

**4.** If you prefer warm tortillas, heat them in a separate pan for a couple of minutes. Place the "chicken" mix on the tortillas, top with parsley, and roll into wraps.

### NOTE

*If you can't find vegan chicken, you can use soy curls (also known as TVP, textured vegetable protein), seitan (which is not gluten-free), or chickpeas instead. If you use soy curls, add them to a pot with boiling water and steep them for 15 minutes off the heat, then drain, before using them in this recipe.*

"Pedro Navaja" by Rubén Blades and Willie Colón

I Don't Want Salad

WRAPS & SANDWICHES

30

# CRISPY
# FRIED TOFU
# SANDWICH

In collaboration with

Nkoyo Adakama, CEO/founder of
Don't Be Chick'n

Yield: 4 sandwiches

*Prep time: 1 day (to allow time to
freeze and thaw twice)
Cook time: 6 to 8 minutes
Total time: 1 day plus 6 to 8 minutes*

With her Oakland-based vegan food truck Don't Be Chick'n, Nkoyo Adakama is on a mission to revolutionize comfort food by offering vegan alternatives that put a spin on those homestyle favorites we all love. This sandwich, which was created in collaboration with Nkoyo and is inspired by her famous vegan "chick'n" sandwich, is no exception. Did you know that double-freezing tofu takes its texture to a whole other level? Paired with a carefully curated selection of seasonings, this sandwich is crispy and just the right amount of spicy.

If you're ever in the Oakland area, be sure to stop by Nkoyo's food truck to try one of her many vegan creations.

## FOR THE SPICY MAYO SPREAD
½ cup (120 mL) vegan mayonnaise

1 tablespoon hot sauce (optional)

½ teaspoon paprika

½ teaspoon garlic powder

## FOR THE FILLING
1 18-ounce (500 g) package medium-firm tofu

1 quart (1 L) high-heat neutral vegetable oil

## FOR THE WET MIX
1 cup (240 mL) soy milk

1 tablespoon apple cider vinegar

1 cup (125 g) all-purpose flour

1 cup (240 mL) sparkling water

1 tablespoon vegan chicken stock powder (or 1½ teaspoons vegan chicken seasoning)

## FOR THE DRY MIX
2 cups (250 g) all-purpose flour

½ cup (60 g) cornstarch

2 teaspoons sea salt

1½ teaspoons smoked paprika

1½ teaspoons mustard powder

1 tablespoon garlic powder

2 teaspoons onion powder

1 teaspoon celery salt

1 teaspoon ground ginger

1½ teaspoons dried thyme

1½ teaspoons dried oregano

1½ teaspoons ground black pepper

½ teaspoon ground white pepper

¼ teaspoon cayenne pepper

## TO SERVE
1 tablespoon vegan butter

4 vegan brioche buns or seeded buns

Sliced pickles

Shredded lettuce or slaw

1. **For the spicy mayo spread:** In a small bowl, whisk the mayonnaise, hot sauce (if using), paprika, and garlic powder until well blended. Refrigerate until ready to use.

2. **For the tofu:** Remove the block of tofu from its package, drain it, and freeze it in a reusable airtight container. Once the tofu is frozen, remove it from the freezer and allow it to defrost. Press the tofu to remove excess liquid, then freeze, defrost, and press it one more time using a tofu press or by wrapping it in a kitchen towel and pressing it between two cutting boards. Double freezing it is necessary to create the right texture and layers in the tofu.

I Don't Want Salad

**WRAPS & SANDWICHES**

*CONTINUES*

**3.** Gently tear the tofu into 8 rectangular pieces (you'll need 2 pieces per sandwich). Mix the milk and apple cider vinegar in a bowl to form buttermilk, then stir in the other wet-mix ingredients using a whisk. Combine the dry mix ingredients in another bowl while you heat the oil in a large pot or a deep fryer over medium heat until it reaches 350°F (180°C). The correct temperature will ensure the tofu pieces get crispy and golden.

**4. Once the oil is hot enough, coat your tofu:** individually dip the pieces in the wet mix, then the dry mix, then the wet mix, then the dry mix again. Coating the tofu twice in each mix will allow for the crispiest result.

**5.** Using a slotted spoon or spatula, place the battered tofu into the hot oil and let fry until golden brown on each side, 6 to 8 minutes. Place the fried tofu on a paper towel to absorb any excess oil.

**6. To assemble the sandwiches:** Melt the vegan butter in a medium-large skillet over medium heat.

**7.** Place the buns face down in the skillet and toast until golden and slightly crisp, 2 to 3 minutes (or a bit longer if you like your buns extra toasty).

**8.** Next, layer the spicy mayo generously on the buns, top and bottom.

**9.** Top with sliced pickles, lettuce or slaw, and your crispy fried tofu and enjoy!

♫ **"Got to Give It Up"** by Marvin Gaye

> **"These are some of the best sandwiches I have ever had, and I've had a lot of sandwiches."**
> —DANIEL RINGKAMP, *one of this cookbook's (unofficial) recipe testers*

# TERRI'S "FISH" FILLET SANDWICH

In collaboration with

Craig Cochran from NuLeaf Restaurant in New York City

Yield: 4 sandwiches

Prep time: 15 minutes
Soak time: 8 hours
(optional; see below)
Cook time: 10 to 15 minutes
Total time: 8 hours soaking,
plus 25 to 30 minutes

When I first moved to New York City in 2014, I fell in love with the world of vegan comfort-food restaurants. After years of living in places with limited vegan dining options, I was in heaven. One of my favorites, Terri, was run by my friend Craig Cochran. My favorite menu item was the vegan fish fillet sandwich made with cashews and heart of palm, a creamy tartar sauce, and melted cheddar-style vegan cheese, all wrapped in a soft bun. At one point, I lived in the same neighborhood as the restaurant and would stop by to get this sandwich at least once or twice a month; it was that good. Terri no longer exists (Craig now has a new restaurant called NuLeaf), but thanks to Craig, the sandwich lives on in this book so you can try it too.

- 1 14-ounce (400 g) can hearts of palm
- ½ cup (70 g) cashews, soaked in water to cover for 8 hours or overnight, then drained (see Notes)
- 3 to 4 tablespoons water
- ½ teaspoon sea salt, or to taste
- 4 cracks fresh black pepper or ¼ teaspoon ground black pepper
- ½ teaspoon Old Bay seasoning
- ¼ teaspoon cayenne pepper
- ¼ cup (30 g) all-purpose flour, gluten-free if desired (see Notes)
- ¼ cup (60 mL) high-heat neutral vegetable oil for frying (preferably not olive oil), or as needed

*FOR THE TARTAR SAUCE*
- ½ cup (120 mL) vegan mayonnaise
- ½ cup (70 g) finely chopped dill pickles
- ½ teaspoon lemon juice
- 2 teaspoons minced white or yellow onion
- Salt and pepper to taste

*TO SERVE*
- 4 vegan burger buns, gluten-free if desired
- 4 vegan cheddar-style cheese slices
- Lettuce leaves (optional)

**GFO**

I Don't Want Salad

WRAPS & SANDWICHES

*CONTINUES*

35

1. Drain the hearts of palm and cut them lengthwise into very thin strips, until the hearts of palm look shredded. This doesn't have to be perfect, but the strips will give you a fleshier texture.

2. Place the soaked cashews in the blender and add the water to cover them. Add the salt, pepper, Old Bay, and cayenne and blend the cashews until smooth. Add the flour and blend again.

3. Transfer the mixture to a bowl, mix with the heart of palm strips, and form into 4 patties with your hands.

4. Heat the oil in a skillet over medium-low heat. Add the patties and fry on each side until golden, 3 to 4 minutes per side (see Notes).

5. Mix the tartar sauce ingredients and set aside.

6. To assemble, spread the tartar sauce on the buns, then add the lettuce, patties, and cheddar-style cheese to make 4 sandwiches. If you want the cheese to melt a bit, wrap each sandwich in aluminum foil for a few minutes; the cheese should melt on its own. Or, top the patties with the cheese as they finish cooking.

## NOTES

• If you don't have time to soak the cashews, you can simply boil them for 5 minutes, then rinse them with cold water and drain.

• You can use gluten-free flours, but make sure they will bind when heated (those with added xanthan or guar gum, for instance).

• You can also bake the patties if you want to avoid frying, but I recommend still using some oil so they crisp on the outside. Place the patties on a baking tray lined with parchment paper, brush both sides with a little oil, and bake at 350°F (180°C) until they're somewhat firm, 15 to 20 minutes.

• I usually make the patties thinner when using larger buns (which is how the original sandwich was served at Terri's Restaurant), or a bit thicker when using small buns like the ones shown in this picture.

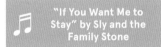
"If You Want Me to Stay" by Sly and the Family Stone

WRAPS & SANDWICHES

# JALAPEÑO POPPER GRILLED CHEESE

Yield: 2 sandwiches

*Prep time: 5 minutes*
*Cook time: 5 to 10 minutes*
*Total time: 10 to 15 minutes*

The only thing that's better than jalapeño poppers or a grilled cheese is a jalapeño popper grilled cheese. The combo of vegan cream cheese and melted cheese simply brings it all to the next level, which is probably also why this easy recipe was one of the recipe testers' absolute favorites. If you don't love spicy food, simply swap out the jalapeños for chopped bell peppers!

½ cup (120 mL) vegan cream cheese, nut-free if desired

1 tablespoon chopped fresh chives

1 or 2 jalapeños, very finely chopped or sliced (see Note)

1 teaspoon garlic powder

1 teaspoon onion powder

1 pinch of sea salt

1 pinch of ground black pepper

1 tablespoon vegan butter

1 cup (100 g) vegan cheese shreds, such as cheddar and mozzarella style, nut-free if desired

4 slices sourdough bread, gluten-free if desired (if your slices are very big, you can use 2 and cut them in half)

**1.** Mix the cream cheese, chives, jalapeño, garlic powder, onion powder, and salt and pepper in a small bowl using a fork or spoon. Set aside.

**2.** Place about half the vegan butter in a large nonstick pan set over medium-high heat.

**3.** Once the butter is melted and the pan is hot, add the vegan cheese shreds to the pan in two piles (about ½ cup/50 g each) in the shape of the bread slices.

**4.** While the cheese is melting, spread the cream cheese mixture onto each of the 4 bread slices (about 2 tablespoons per slice).

**5.** Once the cheese is melted, top each pile with a slice, cream cheese side facing down, and gently press down.

**6.** Using a turner, carefully flip the bread and cheese, add a little more butter to the pan, and then place the remaining two slices on top (cream cheese side facing down). Gently press down again and cook for 1 minute, then flip the whole sandwiches and cook for 30 to 60 more seconds on the other side (you want the bread to be toasted and the cheese melted, but the cream cheese shouldn't be too melty).

## NOTE
*Use just 1 jalapeño (and scrape out the seeds) for less heat. You can also cut up a bell pepper wedge instead of jalapeño to make the sandwiches less spicy/ more kid-friendly.*

## SERVING SUGGESTION
*Enjoy with a bowl of soup—for instance, the Roasted Garlic and Butter Bean Soup with Basil & Thyme (page 132).*

 **"Me Prendes" by Eslabon Armado**

 GFO

 TNF

 LV

I Don't Want Salad

**WRAPS & SANDWICHES**

# CHEESY CRUST
# MUSHROOM & SPINACH PIZZA

**Yield: 1 personal pizza**

*Prep time: 30 minutes*
*Rest time: 1 hour*
*Cook time: 15 to 20 minutes*
*Total time: 1 hour, 45 to 50 minutes*

I have yet to meet a person who doesn't love pizza. It is, quite possibly, the perfect food. Here's an easy Pizza Night dough recipe and a few suggested toppings, but feel free to customize and make it your own. You could even double the ingredients and make mini pizzas for a great kid-friendly activity, letting everyone decorate their own pizza (it's fun for adults too!). For the cheese, you can use a store-bought version or my easy Mozzarella-Style Pizza Cheese (page 207). And if you're feeling lazy, simply use store-bought instead of homemade pizza dough!

*FOR THE DOUGH*

½ cup (120 mL) warm water

1 teaspoon active dry yeast

1 teaspoon sugar

1½ cups (187 g) all-purpose flour, spooned in, plus more for kneading (gluten-free if desired)

½ teaspoon sea salt

4½ teaspoons olive oil

¼ teaspoon dried basil (optional)

¼ teaspoon dried oregano (optional)

*FOR THE TOMATO SAUCE*

½ cup (120 mL) tomato puree (passata)

1 pinch of sea salt

2 teaspoons Italian seasoning (see Note)

1 teaspoon sugar or maple syrup

3 garlic cloves, minced

*FOR THE TOPPINGS*

1½ cups (150 g) vegan mozzarella shreds (or Mozzarella-Style Pizza Cheese, page 207)

1 cup (30 g) baby spinach, packed

2.5 ounces (70 g) button or baby bella mushrooms, very thinly sliced

½ cup (75 g) grape tomatoes, halved

½ small red onion, thinly sliced

1 pinch of freshly cracked pepper

Red pepper flakes (optional)

Fresh basil leaves, for serving

**1. Prepare the dough:** In a large bowl, combine the water, yeast, and sugar and let rest for 15 minutes. The surface should be bubbly.

**2.** Add the flour, salt, oil, and dried herbs and stir well to combine. Turn the dough onto a lightly floured surface and knead for 3 to 4 minutes, until it's springy. Return the dough to a lightly oiled bowl, cover the bowl with a damp kitchen towel or plastic wrap, and let rest in a warm place for an hour or until doubled in size.

OTHER MAIN DISHES · I Don't Want Salad

*CONTINUES*

**3.** Preheat the oven to 450°F (230°C) for at least 20 to 30 minutes. (If you're using a pizza stone, preheat it as well. If using a baking sheet, you can preheat the sheet, but this is not necessary.) Punch down the dough to release air pockets, then transfer to the floured surface.

**4.** Using your hands, stretch the dough to form the pizza. If you stretch it into a circle, it should be about 12.5 inches (32 cm) wide (you can of course make it any shape you want).

**5.** Place the dough on a baking sheet or tray and poke holes in the bottom using a fork.

**6.** Fold half of the vegan cheese into the crust's edges to make the cheesy crust.

**7. For the tomato sauce:** Mix all sauce ingredients (you can also use store-bought tomato sauce) and spread over the dough. Then add the toppings and brush the crust with a little olive oil (optional).

**8.** Bake for 15 to 20 minutes, until the sauce is bubbling, the cheese is melted, and the toppings are cooked. Garnish with the basil leaves.

## NOTES

• *If you don't have Italian seasoning, you can replace this amount with ½ teaspoon dried oregano, 1 teaspoon dried basil, and ½ teaspoon dried thyme.*

• *For an extra crispy crust, bake the pizza at 475ºF (250ºC) instead and reduce the baking time by a few minutes.*

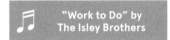
"Work to Do" by The Isley Brothers

# MUSHROOM & GUINNESS PIE

In collaboration with bestselling cookbook authors Henry Firth and Ian Theasby from BOSH TV

**Yield: 4 to 6 servings**

*Prep time: 25 minutes*
*Cook time: 1 hour, 5 minutes to 1 hour, 15 minutes*
*Total time: 1 hour, 30 minutes to 1 hour, 40 minutes*

Henry and Ian are the founders of the world-famous vegan recipe channel BOSH TV. This is their take on a pub classic, and it's incredible! The mushrooms give it a rich and meaty texture that goes perfectly with Guinness's dark umami flavor. Enjoy this on a chilly fall or winter night with your favorite veggies or on its own.

1 18-ounce (500 g) block dairy-free puff pastry or 2 9-ounce (250 g) puff pastry rounds (see Note)

1½ pounds (700 g) cremini or chestnut mushrooms

3 tablespoons olive oil

Sea salt and ground black pepper to taste

4 yellow or white onions, thinly sliced

6 garlic cloves, finely chopped

3 sprigs fresh rosemary, plus extra to garnish

3 sprigs fresh thyme

1 tablespoon light brown sugar

1¼ cups (300 mL) Guinness or other stout or brown ale

2 tablespoons plus 1½ teaspoons all-purpose flour, plus extra for dusting

1 to 2 tablespoons Dijon mustard, to taste

1 tablespoon plus 1 teaspoon dark soy sauce

2 tablespoons vegan butter or margarine

**1.** Line a 9-inch (23 cm) deep-dish pie plate with one half of the puff pastry (roll it out first if using a pastry block).

**2.** Preheat the oven to 350°F (180°C) and line a baking tray with parchment paper.

**3.** Quarter the mushrooms and spread them over the lined baking tray. Drizzle with 1 tablespoon of the oil, season lightly with salt and pepper, and roast for 15 minutes. When the mushrooms are golden and slightly shriveled, remove and set aside, reserving any juices.

**4.** Meanwhile, warm the remaining 2 tablespoons oil in a large frying pan. Add the onions and garlic and cook for 10 minutes over medium heat, stirring occasionally, until softened. Reduce the heat to medium-low.

**5.** Remove the leaves from the rosemary and thyme by running your thumb and forefinger from the top to the base of the stems (the leaves should easily come away). Finely chop the leaves, discarding the stems. Add to the pan along with the sugar and cook for 10 more minutes, until the onions are golden.

I Don't Want Salad

OTHER MAIN DISHES

*CONTINUES*

**6.** Pour the Guinness into the pan, bring to a simmer, and cook for 10 more minutes to reduce the liquid. Reduce the heat to low and add the mushrooms and any juices from the tray. Add the flour, mustard, and soy sauce and simmer gently for 15 to 20 minutes, stirring regularly. Taste and adjust the seasoning, adding more salt, pepper, mustard, or soy sauce if you like. Let cool slightly, then spoon the mushroom mixture into the pie dish lined with puff pastry.

**7.** Lightly dust a work surface with flour and roll out the remaining pastry until it is large enough to cover the top of the pie dish. Brush the rim of the dish with water and lay the pastry over the top. Cut off the excess pastry and crimp the edge either by pinching it between your finger and thumb all the way around, or by pressing it against the dish with the back of a fork.

**8.** Melt the vegan butter in the microwave and use a pastry brush to brush it all over the pastry. Use a small sharp knife to cut a little cross in the center so that steam can escape. Top the crust with a few rosemary sprigs to make it look fancy. Bake for 30 to 35 minutes, until the pastry is golden brown. Serve hot.

**NOTE**

*If using puff pastry rounds (usually about 250 g each), you do not need to roll them out.*

"How Long Do I Have to Wait for You?" by Sharon Jones and the Dap-Kings

TRADITIONAL HOME COOKING

PART TWO

# Cultural Food

PART TWO

TRADITIONAL HOME COOKING

**SO** **MANY CULTURAL DISHES ARE** either easy to veganize or almost vegan to begin with, yet the fear of losing one's cultural foods when going vegan remains. Will I disappoint my parents and/or grandparents if I don't eat their food? Will I become my family's pariah? Is it a sacrifice worth making? These are all very valid questions, and I don't think that minimizing how difficult this transition can seem is helpful. What is helpful, however, is finding a way to merge the two worlds and not underestimating how open-minded people can be, even if it takes a little time for them to adjust.

When I announced to my then seventy-six-year-old grandmother that I was going vegan, she hesitated for a moment, but then said, "You cook it, I eat it. Deal?" She wasn't ready to start cooking vegan herself, but her willingness to at least try my food was a welcome surprise. Other family members had a harder time with my decision, and that's okay. You'll never convince or please everyone, but know that you don't have to give up your favorite meals just because you go vegan. And if you're not vegan, I'd still encourage you to try vegan versions of these meals every once in a while. They might surprise you!

As veganism grows in popularity, so do vegan food blogs. We are now very fortunate to have members of so many different cultures who veganize the dishes they grew up eating and share them with their audiences via blogs, cookbooks, and social media platforms. I have asked some of the people whose work I admire and who I am fortunate to call friends, as well as some of my personal close friends and family, to contribute to this book as I believe that the most authentic way to learn about a culture's food is from members of that culture. That doesn't mean that you can't cook recipes from another culture; on the contrary, making them is encouraged. It just means that if there is a way to celebrate both the food *and* the people who belong to the culture at the same time, it makes the whole experience that much more special. I am beyond honored and grateful to the amazingly talented people who are a part of this cookbook, and I cannot wait for you to meet them all through their recipes.

## Where to Find the Ingredients: Many of the recipes in this chapter
include ingredients that may be hard to find at conventional supermarkets. Please do not let this discourage you from trying them. Exploring stores beyond your supermarket might help you discover a whole new array of ingredients you'll love. Here are a few suggestions for where to shop for them:

**The international section of your supermarket · Asian markets · African and Middle Eastern markets · Central and Latin American markets · Online specialty stores · Farmers markets**

For a full list of recommended markets and online stores, go to bestofvegan.com/mycookbook.

"Being vegan doesn't mean losing your cultural food." —Berto Calkins

# PANFRIED VEGETABLE DUMPLINGS

In collaboration with

WoonHeng Chia, recipe developer (Malaysia)

Yield: 9 large dumplings (about 3 servings)

*Prep time: 25 minutes*
*Rest time: 55 minutes*
*Cook time: 10 minutes*
*Total time: 1 hour, 30 minutes*

SEE PHOTO, PAGES 50–51

This is a new version of one of the most popular recipes we've ever shared on Best of Vegan. Many of WoonHeng's recipes are readers' favorites because, just like these vegetable dumplings, they're so visually appealing and tasty.

"Depending on the regions they're from," WoonHeng tells me, "dumplings, which is a general term used for dough-based wrappers with a savory filling, have different names. The ones I grew up with include *wantan* (*hun tun* or wonton) and *jiao zi*, and these names refer to how the dumpling is prepared. For example, *wantan* has a thinner wrapper, while the latter can have a thicker, chewy dough wrapped around it. There are also different ways of cooking dumplings; common methods include steaming, boiling, panfrying, and frying. You can get super creative with the filling and the dumpling shapes. You may be wondering what a *bao*, or bun, is then. It's also wrapped but often with a dough that has yeast in it, and the most common way to cook it is to steam it. One day, I had run out of yeast and was craving buns, which is how this dumpling wrapper recipe with a bun shape came to life. It's inspired by the daikon radish bun (*luo bo si bing*). This dough, however, uses hot water that allows you to roll it out thinly, which in return creates a crispy outer layer when cooked. They are best served right off the pan with a side of dipping sauce or as is."

*FOR THE DOUGH*

2¼ cups (280 g) all-purpose flour

½ teaspoon sea salt

¾ cup (180 mL) hot water (195°F/90°C)

*FOR THE FILLING*

7 cups (1¼ pounds/600 g) chopped napa cabbage

1 tablespoon plus 1 teaspoon sea salt

1 bunch (1.85 ounces/50 g) of mung bean threads (also known as *fensi*)

1 tablespoon high-heat neutral vegetable oil, plus more for panfrying the dumplings

8 dried shiitake mushrooms (.55 ounce/15 g), rehydrated and thinly sliced

1 small carrot, finely shredded

⅔ cup (85 g) frozen edamame beans, thawed

7 ounces (200 g) firm tofu, drained well

1 tablespoon soy sauce, plus more to taste

½ teaspoon mushroom or umami seasoning

1 tablespoon toasted sesame oil

1 teaspoon sugar

Handful of chopped fresh cilantro leaves

Sesame seeds

*TO SERVE*

Your favorite sauce (such as soy sauce) and/or other condiments

**1. Prepare the dough:** Combine the flour and salt in a large bowl. Using a spatula, stir the flour while adding the hot water until you get a shaggy dough.

**2.** When the dough is cool enough to handle, turn it out onto a lightly floured surface and knead it into a cohesive ball for 3 to 4 minutes. If there are any dry spots of flour left, gradually add cold water, a tablespoon at a time, while kneading. If the dough is sticky, add more flour instead, a tablespoon at a time. Cover the bowl and let rest for 10 minutes.

**3.** Uncover the bowl and knead the dough on a lightly floured surface to get a smooth texture.

**4.** Return the dough to the bowl and cover to let it rest for 30 minutes.

**5. Prepare the filling:** Place the cabbage in a large bowl and rub the leaves generously with the tablespoon of salt to draw the water out of it. Cover and let sit for at least 10 minutes.

**6.** Meanwhile, soak the mung bean threads in warm water and cover for 5 minutes, or until they are pliable but not too soft. Drain the threads and cut them into short pieces, ½ to 1 inch (1.25 to 2.5 cm) long, with a pair of scissors or a knife. Set aside.

**7.** Heat a nonstick skillet with the tablespoon of oil. Sauté the mushrooms until they turn slightly golden and aromatic. Add the carrot and stir-fry for another few seconds, followed by the edamame. Transfer to a large bowl.

**8.** Transfer the cabbage to a large towel or cheesecloth and squeeze out all the water. Do this in two batches if needed. You should have 1¼ to 2 cups (the volume of a 300 to 480 mL container) of cabbage.

**9.** Add the cabbage to the bowl with the mushrooms. Add the tofu along with the reserved mung bean threads.

**10.** Season with the soy sauce, mushroom seasoning, sesame oil, sugar, and the 1 teaspoon salt. Using your fingers, squeeze to mash the tofu while combining all the ingredients until the seasonings are well incorporated.

**11.** Fold in the chopped cilantro, set the bowl aside, and turn your attention to the dough.

**12. Make the dumplings:** Divide the dough into 9 equal portions and roll into balls. Work with one ball at a time and cover the rest with a damp kitchen towel.

**13.** Place a ball on a lightly floured work surface and flatten it with your palm. Roll it into a circle 5 to 6 inches (12.5 to 15 cm) in diameter, aiming to keep the middle part thicker and the edges thinner.

**14.** Place 2 to 3 tablespoons (80 g) of filling in the middle of the circle, bring the sides up to the middle, and pinch to seal all the openings together, creating a round dumpling.

**15.** Place the dumpling between your palms and gently compress and mold it to about ½ to 1 inch (1.25 to 2.5 cm) in height. Repeat with the remaining dough until you have 9 large dumplings. Brush the smooth side with water and sprinkle sesame seeds on top, then gently press to adhere.

**16.** Heat a large nonstick skillet over medium heat and add a drizzle of oil.

**17.** Place the dumplings in the pan, seeded side down, in one layer, spaced slightly apart. Panfry until golden brown on the first side, about 2 to 3 minutes, cooking in batches if needed.

**18.** Flip the dumplings, cover with a lid (preferably one with a vent), and cook over low heat until they start to puff up, 3 to 5 minutes. (See Note.) Continue to panfry until golden brown on this second side, adding more oil if needed.

**19.** To check if they're done, press the outside of a dumpling. If it bounces back, it's ready. Serve immediately with your favorite sauce or condiments.

## NOTE

*For softer-textured dumplings, once the sesame sides turn golden brown, flip and add about ¾ cup (180 mL) water to the pan. Cover with a lid and steam until all the water has evaporated, 3 to 5 minutes.*

"You & Me" by 菲道尔

# DUMPLING FAQS

**1** **How to avoid making the sealed bottom too thick**
When you roll out the dough, aim to get thin edges with a thicker middle. Then when you seal the edges together, forming the bottom, it will be the same thickness as the top. Alternatively, you can shape the dumplings into half-moons by simply folding the dough in half over the filling.

**2** **How to store the dumplings**
VERSION 1: Freeze the dumplings in an airtight container after you've formed them but before cooking. When you're ready to eat, follow the same steps for cooking the dumplings—no thawing needed—but add water to steam them, ensuring the insides are fully cooked.

VERSION 2: Freeze the dumplings after you've cooked them. The best way to reheat them is to steam or microwave them (again, no need to thaw). If using a microwave, cover the dumplings with a damp kitchen towel and microwave for 1 to 2 minutes.

# CHINESE VEGETABLE DUMPLINGS

In collaboration with
Christine Wong, author,
eco-conscious cook,
and freelance digital
content creator

Yield: About 36 dumplings

Prep time: 1 hour
Rest time: 20 minutes
Cook time: 20 minutes
Total time: 1 hour, 40 minutes

Dumplings are an incredibly versatile food. In contrast with the panfried vegetable dumplings, here's a more classic Chinese version by Christine Wong. Christine is someone whose work I've long admired, and when it comes to dumplings, hers are among the very best. She even teaches workshops on how to make them both in New York City and online. Here's a bit more about this recipe in her words:

"[While] growing up in Hong Kong, dumplings literally [became] a part of me! From bustling dim sum banquet halls to a simple bowl of wonton noodles at an outdoor food stall, they now evoke nostalgia. These little wrapped parcels are pure comfort to me and are one of the first Chinese recipes I recreated when I moved to New York City in 2002. What I love about dumplings is that they're so versatile; you can stuff them with anything (even leftovers!), and they can be cooked any number of ways—boiled, steamed, panfried, and even deep-fried! While I'm still working on veganizing more specific dim sum, the recipe I am honored to share with Best of Vegan is the one I've been making since that very first time I made them. This is also the recipe that I use to teach hundreds of people in my hands-on dumpling classes. Enjoy!"

*FOR THE FILLING*

4½ teaspoons olive oil

1 cup (450 g) finely diced butternut squash

1 cup (60 g) finely diced shiitake mushrooms

2 scallions (both white and green parts), finely chopped

2 cups (60 g) finely chopped fresh spinach

½-inch (12 mm) piece of fresh ginger, grated

1 to 2 tablespoons soy sauce, to taste

½ teaspoon sea salt

¼ teaspoon ground white pepper

*FOR THE WRAPPERS*

3 cups (375 g) all-purpose flour

1 teaspoon baking powder

1 teaspoon salt

1 cup (240 mL) just-boiled water (see Note)

1 tablespoon sunflower seed oil

*TO PANFRY THE DUMPLINGS*

4½ teaspoons sunflower seed oil per batch, plus more as needed

¼ cup (60 mL) filtered water per batch

Cultural Food

BITES & SIDES

*CONTINUES*

**1. Make the filling:** Heat a large, dry skillet over high heat and coat the pan with the oil. Add all the filling ingredients and sauté for 5 to 7 minutes, until the moisture from the vegetables evaporates. You don't want the filling to be too wet or your dumpling wrappers will break. Transfer the mixture to a large plate and let it cool before wrapping.

**2. Make the wrappers:** In a large bowl, mix the flour, baking powder, and salt. Stirring continuously, gradually pour in the hot water and oil and stir until the mixture begins to clump together in little clusters. Knead these together until a large ball of dough forms. Turn this out onto a clean work surface and knead for 10 more minutes, or until the dough becomes smooth and elastic (like Play-Doh). If it's sticky and too wet, add another tablespoon or two of flour. If it's too dry, add another tablespoon of hot water or oil. Cover the dough with a clean, damp kitchen towel and set aside for 20 minutes.

**3.** On a clean, lightly floured work surface, roll the wrapper dough into a long, skinny piece about 1 inch in diameter and divide it into approximately 36 equal pieces. Keep these covered with a kitchen towel while you assemble the dumplings.

**4.** Have a seat and get comfortable at a clean, dry work surface. Invite a few friends or family members to join in on the fun!

**5. Assemble the dumplings:** Flatten and roll each piece into a ⅛-inch (3 mm) thick round, about 3 to 4 inches (7.5 to 10 cm) in diameter. Place the wrapper in the palm of your hand. Scoop one teaspoonful of the filling onto the center of the dough round; take care not to overfill it, or it'll be difficult to close. Fold the wrapper in half—into a semicircle—and firmly pinch the edges together to seal (you can then pinch pleats or folds, although that isn't necessary). Place the assembled dumpling onto a parchment-lined baking tray and continue until you run out of wrappers or filling.

**6. Panfry the dumplings:** Warm a large, dry skillet over high heat. Coat the pan with the oil. Place the dumplings in a single layer, making sure not to overcrowd them (work in batches if necessary, using more oil and water for each batch). Crisp up the bottoms of the dumplings for 3 to 5 minutes. Reduce the heat to medium, carefully add ¼ cup (60 mL) water, cover with a tight-fitting lid, and cook for 6 minutes, until the wrappers are steamed through and the water has been absorbed. Remove the lid, drizzle another teaspoon of the oil into the pan, and crisp up the bottoms again for another 2 to 4 minutes.

## NOTES

• *For colorful dough, replace the boiled water with fresh-pressed juices or teas (e.g., blue butterfly pea flower tea, carrot juice, or beetroot juice, brought to a boil), or add 2 teaspoons turmeric for yellow dough, spirulina powder for green. Alternatively, vegan food coloring can be used as well. You can divide the wrapper recipe into thirds or sixths for multiple colors in one batch.*

• *Make a big batch of these dumplings/potstickers and store them in the freezer for an easy anytime meal. Making the dough from scratch allows you to make a variety of fun folds, and you can also color them with food ingredients.*

"的就是你" ("I love you") by Leehom Wang

# WELSH RAREBITS

In collaboration with
Gaz Oakley from Avant-Garde
Vegan, chef and bestselling author

Yield: 4 servings

*Prep time: 15 minutes*
*Rest time: 15 minutes*
*Cook time: 35 minutes*
*Total time: 1 hour, 5 minutes*

Gaz Oakley is a vegan chef from Wales in southwest Great Britain, which is known for its stunning scenery, with a distinctive Welsh language, and Celtic culture. This recipe is a simple dish consisting of toasted bread covered in melted cheese and ale and topped with mustard.

According to Gaz, this dish has been eaten in Wales since at least the 1500s under the name *caws pobi*, which is Welsh for "toasted cheese." "Welsh rarebit has humble beginnings—like most things in Wales," he tells me. "Welsh peasants used cheese as a substitute for the meat they could not afford."

## FOR THE "CHEESE" TOPPING

- ½ cup (70 g) raw cashews
- ½ cup (120 mL) cold plant milk
- 3 tablespoons tapioca starch
- 3 tablespoons nutritional yeast
- 1 teaspoon prepared yellow or Dijon mustard
- 1 teaspoon white miso paste
- 3 tablespoons beer, preferably Welsh (ales and light and dark beers also work)
- 1 pinch of sea salt
- 1 pinch of ground white pepper
- ¼ teaspoon onion powder
- ½ cup (120 mL) cold filtered water

## FOR THE CARAMELIZED RED ONIONS

- 2 tablespoons high-heat neutral vegetable oil
- 3 red onions, halved and thinly sliced
- ¼ cup (50 g) coconut sugar or brown sugar
- 3 tablespoons balsamic vinegar
- 1 pinch of sea salt
- 1 pinch of ground black pepper
- 2 sprigs fresh thyme, leaves chopped

## TO SERVE

- 1 baguette, cut into thick slices on an angle and toasted
- Prepared yellow or Dijon mustard

1. Set your oven to broil to preheat it.

2. **Make the "cheese":** Quick-soak the nuts by popping them in a heatproof bowl and covering with boiling water. Let soften for around 15 minutes.

3. **Meanwhile, make the caramelized onions:** In a heavy-bottomed saucepan set over medium heat, add the oil followed by the onions. Cook for 3 to 4 minutes, stirring often, until they start to soften and color. Add the sugar, vinegar, salt and pepper, and thyme. Stir well and turn the heat down very low. Cover the saucepan and allow the onions to caramelize for 15 minutes. Stir them or shake the pan every now and then.

4. Once the nuts have softened, drain and place them in a high-speed blender with the remaining "cheese" ingredients. Blend on high speed until you have a smooth mixture.

5. Pour the mixture into a nonstick saucepan and, using a spatula, start stirring over medium heat. Be patient—you will be stirring for around 8 minutes. Stir until the topping is thick but still pourable.

6. **To assemble:** Arrange the toasted bread slices on a parchment-lined baking tray and generously top each slice with cheese mix. Place the pan on the top rack of the oven and broil for 3 to 4 minutes or until browned. Serve straightaway with plenty of caramelized red onions and your favorite mustard.

"Memphis Soul Stew" by King Curtis

# IVORIAN ATTIÉKÉ

In collaboration with
Kayatou "Kady" Konaté (Ivory Coast)

Yield: 5 to 6 servings

*Prep time: 20 minutes*
*Cook time: 12 minutes*
*Total time: 32 minutes*

*Attiéké* is a very common and popular dish in Ivory Coast, where Kady, who is both a friend and my cousin's wife, is originally from. Its base is cassava, which is a staple you'll find in most African countries, and it's similar to couscous in look and texture, yet it's naturally gluten-free. It's a simple, beloved staple.

"*Attiéké* also refers to the way we Ivorians prepare it. I consider it an emblem of Ivorian cuisine," Kady tells me. "You can eat it with fish, chicken, or *kedjenou* [spice stew], but if you want to make it vegan, you can serve it with black-eyed peas and fried plantains, which we call *alloco*." Traditionally, making attiéké is quite a lengthy process, as the cassava roots need to be chopped, blended with water, fermented, and dried for several days. We've therefore decided to use dehydrated attiéké here, which you can find online and at most African food stores. If you're interested in seeing how it's traditionally made, go to bestofvegan.com/mycookbook for a step-by-step tutorial.

GF

TNF

HP

Cultural Food

BITES & SIDES

### FOR THE ATTIÉKÉ
1 18-ounce (500 g) package of dehydrated attiéké
1 tablespoon olive oil or other vegetable oil
Sea salt and ground black pepper to taste

### FOR THE SIDE SALAD
2 tablespoons olive oil
2 large tomatoes, chopped
1 onion, diced
3 garlic cloves, minced
½ cucumber, chopped
Juice of 2 lemons (4 tablespoons)
Sea salt and ground black pepper to taste
Chili sauce to taste (optional)

### TO SERVE
3 to 4 cups (500 to 700 g) cooked black-eyed peas, mixed with a homemade tomato sauce (see recipe that follows)
3 to 4 fried plantains (see Congolese "Chicken" Moambé on page 71 for instructions)

**1. Prepare the attiéké:** To rehydrate the attiéké, place it in a bowl with 1⅔ cups (400 mL) hot (almost boiling) water, cover, and let soak for 5 to 8 minutes. Drain, then transfer the attiéké to a steamer pot and steam for about 5 minutes until tender and fluffy.

**2.** Using a fork, mix the steamed attiéké in a bowl with the olive oil, salt, and pepper.

**3. Prepare the salad:** In a medium bowl, mix the ingredients for the side salad.

**4.** Portion out the ingredients into bowls and serve.

## NOTE
*Each of the elements of this dish can be prepared and served as an individual side to accompany other dishes as well.*

"Y'en a Marre" by Tiken Jah Fakoly

58

# Easy Tomato Sauce

2 tablespoons olive oil

2 small to medium onions, finely chopped

4 garlic cloves, minced

1 teaspoon paprika

¼ teaspoon chili powder (optional)

Sea salt to taste

Ground black pepper to taste

2 tablespoons tomato paste

2 large tomatoes, chopped

½ cup (120 mL) water

**1.** Heat the olive oil in a saucepan over medium heat. Sauté the onions and garlic for 5 minutes.

**2.** Add the seasonings, tomato paste, chopped tomatoes, and water.

**3.** Mix and let simmer for 3 to 5 minutes. When thickened, mix the sauce with the black-eyed peas.

Yield: 1 cup

*Prep time: 5 minutes*
*Cook time 10 minutes*
*Total time: 15 minutes*

# NIGERIAN
# AKARA & PAP

In collaboration with

Samantha Onyemenam,
recipe developer and writer
(Nigeria and the UK)

Yield: 5 to 6 servings

*Prep time: 1 day or overnight*
*Cook time: 10 minutes*
*Total time: 1 day, 10 minutes*

Samantha is the creator and author of our Best of Vegan "Culture Tuesday" series, a weekly column that explores different cuisines from around the globe through a vegan and plant-based lens. For this recipe, she's bringing back one of her favorite Nigerian childhood breakfast dishes: Akara & Pap.

"It was one of my favorite things to wake up to the smell of *akara* frying and knowing I was about to have a GOOD breakfast!" Samantha recalls. "I did not like beans as a child, but somehow, *akara* made its way to my heart. Its flavor, warmth, and fluffy texture were undeniably a wonderful experience crowned by the sweet-and-sour flavor of the fermented corn pudding, *pap*, it was always served with. *Akara* and *pap* weren't things I watched being made. They were more like magic that came out of the kitchen. The older I've gotten, the more I have wanted to learn about my culinary culture and know how to make cultural dishes from scratch, especially those I cannot purchase in the UK. I want to keep the magic and experience of *akara* and *pap* in my life and now share it with you as well." The traditional way to make *pap* includes a lengthy process over several days. This recipe, therefore, includes the simplified version using powdered *pap* instead. To see the traditional process, go to bestofvegan.com/mycookbook.

*FOR THE AKARA*

1 pound (450 g) dried black-eyed peas soaked overnight

1 medium red onion, cut into chunks

1 to 2 Scotch bonnet peppers, to taste

1½ teaspoons (5 g) fresh ginger, chopped

2 0.35-ounce (10 g) vegetable stock cubes

4 to 6 tablespoons (60 to 80 mL) water

Sea salt to taste

High-heat neutral vegetable oil, for frying

*FOR THE PAP*

6 heaped tablespoons powdered pap

2 cups (480 mL) cold water

2 to 2½ cups (480 to 600 mL) freshly boiled water

*TO SERVE*

Sugar to taste

Vegan evaporated milk (such as Nature's Charm evaporated coconut milk), optional

GFO

TNF

HP

Cultural Food

BITES & SIDES

*CONTINUES*

1.  **For the akara:** Peel the soaked beans (but, see Notes) by rubbing them between your hands over a bowl. To get rid of the peels, fill the bowl of beans with water, shake the beans around, then pour the water out. The peels will be floating on top of the water and will drain away.

2.  In a blender, combine the peeled beans, onion, peppers, ginger, vegetable stock cubes, 4 tablespoons (60 mL) water, and salt to taste (work in batches if necessary). Pulse to break down the beans before fully blending (see Notes). Add up to 2 more tablespoons water if needed; do not use more water than specified as the akara paste needs to be thick for the akara to rise and not disintegrate when fried.

3.  Using an electric whisk or the whisk attachment of a stand mixer, incorporate air into the batter until it is fluffy. This ensures that the akara floats as it fries and the interior cooks to the right texture. If the batter is very smooth, whisk until it almost forms stiff peaks.

4.  Pour oil into a large pot and heat to roughly 335°F (170°C).

5.  Using an oiled tablespoon, scoop some of the mixture into the oil. Repeat with 4 more scoops; more than 5 akara might drop the temperature of the oil too much.

6.  Fry the akara until both sides are brown, turning halfway through. This should take roughly 5 minutes. Repeat until all the batter has been used up. Drain on paper towels to remove excess oil, then prepare the pap.

**(The following should be carried out after the akara is cooked)**

1.  **For the pap:** In a pot or saucepan, dissolve the powdered pap in the cold water.

2.  Pour the freshly boiled water over it gently and stir with a spoon or whisk until the pap begins to thicken.

3.  Place the pot on the stove and turn the heat up to medium-high.

4.  Stir continuously until the pap forms a porridge with a consistency that is slightly thicker than custard.

5.  Take off the heat and serve immediately (with the akara) with sugar to taste and a drizzle of vegan evaporated milk on top.

## NOTES

• *Akara can be made without peeling the beans. However, traditionally the beans are peeled. Unpeeled beans result in an akara with a slightly gray interior and flecks of dark bits on the exterior. The texture will be less fluffy but the taste remains the same.*

• *For a smooth akara paste, use a high-speed blender. If you don't have one, make the mixture in smaller batches and use the pulse function to break down the beans as much as possible before fully blending. Akara made using a less powerful blender will have a less smooth texture.*

"River" by Ibeyi

# PUERTO RICAN RICE TWO WAYS

**In collaboration with**

Gabriel Ocasio-Cortez, activist for Deaf and hard of hearing inclusivity and content accessibility, founder of the Deaf Collective, and homeless shelter worker

Gabriel grew up in the Bronx, New York, but his family is originally from Puerto Rico. When I asked him which recipes most reminded him of his childhood, he immediately told me about Sopa de Arroz Con Leche, a type of rice pudding that is a beloved breakfast and dessert in Puerto Rico, and Arroz Amarillo, yellow rice. Gabriel, who is not fully vegan, has tried going vegan in the past, but always found it challenging—partly for himself, but mostly for others, with accessibility and affordability being major concerns. How do you advocate for a lifestyle that not everyone can afford? An excellent and important question. One way to make it more accessible and affordable is to provide options and resources for people. Another way is to create and share recipes that cost less to make by using staple foods like rice, which can be bought in bulk.

One more area in which Gabriel fights for accessibility is through his nonprofit organization the Deaf Collective, which supports Deaf and queer communities by providing educational materials for everyone and grants for those in need.

## Sopa de Arroz Con Leche
### PUERTO RICAN RICE PUDDING

1 tablespoon vegan butter

1 cup (200 g) raw, short-grain white rice

3 cups (720 mL) water

½ teaspoon sea salt, or to taste

2 cups (480 mL) unsweetened oat milk or cashew milk, plus more if needed

**1.** Melt the butter in a medium pot over medium heat. Wash the rice, then add it to the pot with the water and salt.

**2.** Stir, bring to a boil, and cook for 15 minutes. (Don't stir too much once it's boiling.)

**3.** Once all the water has evaporated, add the milk and stir. Reduce the heat to low and simmer for another 15 to 20 minutes.

**4.** Taste and add more salt or milk if needed.

### NOTE

*Sopa de Arroz Con Leche is supposed to be creamy with a bit of a salty taste, which differs from other cultures' sweeter and somewhat firmer variations that often also include additional flavors like cinnamon or vanilla. Although it is not recommended, you may of course add a little maple syrup, cinnamon, or vanilla to adjust this recipe to your liking.*

Yield: 4 servings

*Prep time: 5 minutes*
*Cook time: 30 to 35 minutes*
*Total time: 35 to 40 minutes*

*SEE PHOTO, PAGE 64*

GF

TNF

Cultural Food

BITES & SIDES

*CONTINUES*

Sopa de Arroz
Con Leche
(page 63)

# Arroz Amarillo

PUERTO RICAN YELLOW RICE

**1¼ cups (225 g) uncooked long-grain white rice**

**1 small onion**

**1 green bell pepper**

**2 or 3 sweet or medium chile peppers, like Aleppo or habanero peppers**

**½ handful of fresh cilantro**

**3 garlic cloves**

**3 tablespoons achiote oil or olive oil**

**1 teaspoon turmeric powder or more to taste**

**1 cup (240 mL) crushed tomatoes**

**¼ cup (45 g) chopped pitted green olives**

**2 cups (480 mL) water**

**Sea salt and ground black pepper to taste**

**1.** Wash and cook the rice according to the package instructions, but drain it after half the indicated cooking time and set aside.

**2.** Finely chop the onion, bell pepper, chile peppers, and cilantro and mince the garlic. Heat the oil in a large saucepan over medium heat, add the vegetables and turmeric, and sauté for 5 minutes.

**3.** Add the crushed tomatoes and olives, stir, and cook for another 3 to 4 minutes.

**4.** Add the rice and the water. Bring to a boil, reduce the heat to medium-low, and add salt and pepper to taste. Cover and simmer for 15 to 20 minutes, until the water is absorbed.

Yield: 4 servings

*Prep time: 20 minutes*
*Cook time: 25 to 30 minutes*
*Total time: 45 to 50 minutes*

"Ríe y Llora" by Celia Cruz

Cultural Food

**BITES & SIDES**

# PÃO DE QUEIJO
## (Brazilian Cheese Bread)

**In collaboration with**
Luisa Possas and Fernanda Feher

**Yield: 4 servings**
*Prep time: 15 minutes*
*Cook time: 40 minutes*
*Total time: 55 minutes*

Pão de Queijo, which literally translates to "bread of cheese," originated during slavery times in the Brazilian state of Minas Gerais. The cassava root, also known as manioc, yuca, or tapioca, was peeled, grated, and cooked by Portuguese colonizers. The residue from this process, essentially tapioca starch, was gathered by enslaved people, who then formed it into balls and baked it. After slavery ended in Brazil in 1888, people started adding milk and cheese to the recipe, turning it into what is still known as Pão de Queijo. It's something that every Brazilian household makes and eats regularly There are even entire stores, like A Casa do Pão de Queijo ("the house of cheese bread"), dedicated to it.

Fernanda, one of my closest friends whom I've known for over twenty years, was the first person to introduce me to Brazilian culture and cuisine. I later stayed with her and her family in Brazil for a few months and got to eat Pão de Queijo almost every day during my time there. She and another Brazilian friend of ours, Luisa, went vegan a few years ago and thus began our quest to veganize the Brazilian classics they grew up with and I had grown to love as well. This recipe is a favorite that was created in Luisa's kitchen.

- 10.5 ounces (300 g) potatoes or arracacha root, peeled (see Notes), cubed
- 1½ cups (187.5 g) sweet tapioca flour (*polvilho doce*, Yoki is a common brand; see Notes)
- ½ cup (62.5 g) sour tapioca flour (*polvilho azedo*, Yoki is a common brand; see Notes) (if using)
- 1 teaspoon active dry yeast
- 2 tablespoons nutritional yeast
- 1 teaspoon garlic powder
- ½ cup (120 mL) water
- 5 tablespoons neutral vegetable oil
- 1 teaspoon salt
- 1 teaspoon prepared yellow or Dijon mustard (optional)

**1.** Preheat the oven to 350°F (180°C). Line a baking tray with parchment paper.

**2.** Cook the potato in boiling water until soft, 15 to 20 minutes. Drain and, when cool enough to handle, mash until it turns into a puree.

**3.** Mix the tapioca flours, dry yeast, nutritional yeast, and garlic powder in a large bowl.

**4.** Bring the water, oil, and salt to a boil in a small pan, then pour it into the starch mixture. Mix using a fork until you get a crumbly consistency. When it starts looking like a dough, mix in the potato puree and mustard (if using) until the dough turns smooth. If it's too dry or crumbly, add a splash more water and knead it into the dough.

**5.** Form little dough balls and place them on the prepared baking tray. (If you want to make these in advance, you can also freeze them at this point for later use.)

**6.** Bake for 20 to 22 minutes or until light golden.

## NOTES

- *Arracacha is a root vegetable that is also known as either* mandioquinha *("little cassava") or* batata-baroa. *Arracacha is preferred in this recipe, but may be hard to find, in which case you can use equal amounts of either potatoes, sweet potatoes, or cassava root instead.*

- *Brazilians use a mix of sweet and sour tapioca flours, but if you can't find these, you may just use 2 cups (230 g) of regular tapioca flour.*

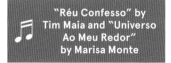
"Réu Confesso" by Tim Maia and "Universo Ao Meu Redor" by Marisa Monte

Cultural Food

BITES & SIDES

# BORANI BANJAN
## (Afghan Eggplant Dish)

In collaboration with

Aiescha Darmal

Yield: 4 servings as a side dish

*Prep time: 25 minutes*
*Cook time: 55 minutes*
*Total time: 1 hour, 20 minutes*

Aiescha is a close friend of mine whose love for her Afghan roots translates to everything she does. We met while living next door to each other in college fifteen years ago. We would often share meals while talking about our families. Aiescha's parents were political refugees who left Afghanistan a month before she was born. They raised her, and later her sisters, to be proud Afghan women, always honoring their culture by teaching them to speak Dari, cooking Afghan feasts, and listening to Afghan music. "One thing about Afghan people," Aiescha tells me, "is we're very proud to be Afghan." The star of this dish, Borani Banjan—one of Aiescha's favorites—is eggplant. It's a flavorful and incredibly delicious side dish that could win over even those who don't usually love eggplant. It's certainly become a new favorite of mine too.

 **Playlist: "Shaparak" by Samir Rohesh**

*FOR THE GARLIC MINT YOGURT SAUCE*
1½ cups (340 mL) unsweetened vegan yogurt

2 to 3 large garlic cloves, minced

Juice of ½ lemon

¼ teaspoon sea salt

1 teaspoon dried mint

¼ teaspoon dried dill (optional)

*FOR THE EGGPLANT*
4 small eggplant (about 28 ounces/800 g), sliced into ½-inch (1.25 cm) discs (see Notes)

1 tablespoon sea salt

6 to 7 cups (1½ to 1¾ L) water (to soak the eggplant in)

¼ cup (60 mL) neutral high-heat vegetable oil, or more as needed

*FOR THE TOMATO SAUCE*
1 tablespoon olive oil

1 medium red onion, finely chopped

2 garlic cloves, minced

½ teaspoon sea salt, or to taste

¼ teaspoon ground black pepper, or to taste

½ teaspoon turmeric powder

¼ teaspoon cumin powder

½ teaspoon chili powder

¼ teaspoon paprika (optional)

¼ teaspoon ground coriander (optional)

2 medium tomatoes, chopped

1 tablespoon tomato paste

¼ cup (60 mL) water, plus more if needed

*OTHER INGREDIENTS*
3 medium tomatoes, sliced

1 green or red bell pepper, chopped

*FOR THE TURMERIC TOPPING*
2 tablespoons olive oil

¾ teaspoon turmeric powder

2 whole red dried chiles

1 tablespoon dried mint

*TO SERVE*
Garlic mint yogurt sauce

Turmeric topping

Cracked black pepper

Fresh mint leaves, chopped

Afghan bread (or similar bread)

1. **Make the yogurt sauce:** Mix all yogurt sauce ingredients in a small bowl using a whisk or a fork. Place in the fridge until ready to serve.

2. **Make the eggplant:** Place the sliced eggplant in a large bowl and rub them with the salt. Fill the bowl with the water and let soak for 15 to 30 minutes while you make the tomato sauce and prepare the remaining vegetables.

3. **Make the tomato sauce:** Heat the olive oil in a saucepan over medium heat. Add the onion and sauté for 3 minutes. Add the garlic and spices and cook for 1 more minute before adding the chopped tomatoes, tomato paste, and water. Mix and cook for 3 to 5 more minutes, adding 2 to 3 more tablespoons of water if necessary.

4. **Continue to prepare the eggplant:** Drain and discard the water from the eggplant slices, then squeeze out any excess water from each slice using your hands.

**5.** Heat ¼ cup (60 mL) neutral oil (or more as needed) in a large nonstick skillet over medium heat. Add the eggplant slices and sauté for 10 minutes, flipping halfway through. The eggplant should start to get golden brown, but not be burned. If you're not using a nonstick skillet, you may need to add more oil and/or flip the slices more often. Place them on paper or kitchen towels to absorb excess oil.

**6.** **Now it's time to bring the Borani Banjan together:** To a large, wide-mouthed pot or pan (similar to a wok), add a very thin layer of tomato sauce (you'll need 3 layers total), a layer each of eggplant, a layer of sliced tomatoes and chopped bell peppers, another thin layer of tomato sauce, another layer of eggplant and vegetables, topped with one final layer of tomato sauce. Add a lid and cook over medium-low heat for 30 to 35 minutes. No need to stir, but check about every 10 minutes to ensure it's cooking evenly and that nothing is burning.

**7.** Taste and add more salt and/or pepper if needed.

**8.** **Make the topping:** Heat the olive oil in a small skillet and add the turmeric, dried chiles, and mint. Cook for 60 seconds and set aside.

**9.** Transfer the Borani Banjan to a large serving dish and top with a few dollops of yogurt sauce, a drizzle of the turmeric topping, cracked pepper, and fresh mint.

**10.** For each serving, place a layer of yogurt sauce in a small bowl or plate, top with Boran Banjani from the large serving dish, and enjoy with a piece of Afghan bread.

## NOTES

• *If you can't find small eggplant, you can use larger ones and then cut them into smaller pieces before slicing them. If using mini eggplant (they're less than half the size of small eggplant), be sure to weigh them to know how many you need.*

• *The turmeric topping is optional but adds a nice little extra touch.*

• *A tip from Aiescha's mother: You can prepare the tomato sauce using only garlic, onion, salt, and pepper as the main ingredients, omitting the turmeric, cumin, chili, paprika, and coriander, depending on what you have on hand. You'll still get the full flavor of the tomatoes and eggplant.*

# CONGOLESE "CHICKEN" MOAMBÉ

In collaboration with
_____

Johnnie and Maggie Masson (Democratic Republic of the Congo)

Yield: 6 to 8 servings
_____

*Prep time: 30 minutes*
*Cook time: 1 hour*
*Total time: 1 hour, 30 minutes*

This is a recipe my great-grandmother, Lusiyah Pousambi, used to make for my grandmother Maggie and great-uncle Johnnie before they were taken from her. During Belgium's colonial regime in what is now the Democratic Republic of the Congo, children born to Congolese mothers and European or Asian fathers were seen as a problem that needed solving, and so they were often separated from their mothers and sent to boarding schools in Europe or across the Congo. Some even had their names changed and were given up for adoption without their mother's consent. Growing up, I was told that when Maggie was two-and-a-half years old and when Johnnie was almost twelve, they were each sent to live and be educated in religious boarding schools in Belgium, never to see their mother again.

Because Maggie was still so young when she left, the nuns at the boarding school told her that her mother had died. She would occasionally receive letters from her Scottish father, but any reference to her mother was concealed by the school. So, when she was fourteen and her father came to visit her in Belgium for the first time, accompanied by her younger brother Johnnie, she was stunned to find out that her mother was still alive. At age twenty she ended up moving back to the Congo, which is where she had and raised my mother, but because of the geographical distance and limited resources, she was unable to find her own mother. Johnnie still has vivid memories of Lusiyah; his favorite ones are of her cooking him plantain beignets and chicken *moambé*, a palm butter dish traditionally served with chicken and cassava leaves. For this recipe, we used vegan chicken instead of regular chicken, which is really the only ingredient that needed to be replaced. When I eat it, I imagine Lusiyah cooking it and wonder how different things could have been if we'd gotten a chance to know her.

> "But there's a story behind everything. How a picture got on a wall. How a scar got on your face. Sometimes the stories are simple, and sometimes they are hard and heartbreaking. But behind all your stories is always your mother's story, because hers is where yours begin."
> —MITCH ALBOM

**GF**

Cultural Food

MAIN DISHES

*CONTINUES*

*FOR THE PILI PILI*
**3 Scotch bonnet peppers**

**1 tablespoon refined coconut oil, melted**

**¼ teaspoon sea salt**

*FOR THE MOAMBÉ*
**2 onions, very finely chopped**

**3 garlic cloves, minced**

**2 tablespoons refined coconut oil**

**28 ounces (800 g) vegan chicken pieces**

**1 tablespoon dried thyme**

**1¼ teaspoon sea salt, or to taste**

**1 teaspoon ground pepper**

**1 28-ounce (800 g) can moambé (palm cream/butter)**

*FOR THE SAKA SAKA*
**1 onion, finely chopped**

**2 to 4 garlic cloves, minced**

**Sea salt and ground black pepper to taste**

**2 14-ounce (400 g) cans saka saka (precooked cassava leaves; see Notes)**

*TO SERVE*
**4 ripe plantains (the peel should be black or almost black)**

**Cooked white rice**

**1. Start by making the pili pili:** (If possible, use surgical gloves for this step, and beware—the Scotch bonnet peppers are so spicy they can make your eyes water.) Cut the peppers open using a sharp knife and discard both the stems and seeds. Roughly chop the peppers and put them in a small food processor. Pulse a few times, until they're finely chopped, then add the melted coconut oil and salt. Pulse again until just combined. Set aside. (See Notes.)

**2. Prepare the vegan chicken:** Sauté the chopped onions and garlic in the coconut oil in a large pan over medium heat for 5 to 7 minutes. Add the vegan chicken pieces, thyme, salt, and pepper, reduce the heat to medium-low, and cook for another 5 to 7 minutes, then set aside.

**3.** Pour the contents of the moambé can into a large pot and cook over medium-low heat (do not stir!) until the palm oil starts rising to the top (10 to 15 minutes). Tilting the pot slightly and using a ladle, carefully remove about three-quarters of the palm oil that's risen to the top and set aside (you'll need it for the saka saka and for frying the plantains).

**4.** Stir the prepared vegan chicken into the moambé, mix, cover, and simmer over medium-low heat for 15 to 20 minutes.

**5. Cook the saka saka**: Sauté the onion and garlic in 1 tablespoon of the palm oil (from the moambé) over medium heat until translucent, 4 to 5 minutes. Season with salt and pepper to taste. Add in the contents of the saka saka cans, mix with the sautéed onion and garlic, and let simmer over medium-low heat for another 5 minutes.

**6.** Peel the plantains and slice them into discs. Heat the remaining palm oil in a large skillet over medium heat, then panfry the plantains in the hot oil until golden and crispy on both sides, 5 to 6 minutes, flipping halfway through cooking time. (You can also fry them in a fryer using vegetable oil.)

**7.** Serve everything together with the pili pili on the side for extra spiciness.

## NOTES

• *If you wish to preserve the pili pili for later, cook it in a small pan or pot over medium to high heat for 1 to 2 minutes and then store it in the fridge. This will make it last longer, about 2 to 3 days. You can also freeze it for even longer.*

• *Canned saka saka is precooked. If you can only find frozen or fresh cassava leaves, these will need to be cooked in water over medium-low heat for about 2 hours, until fully cooked.*

"Ma Mama" by Toto Bona Lokua and "Mamou" by Franco

# MOROCCAN VEGGIE TAJINE KEFTA

**In collaboration with**

Yamina El Atlassi (Morocco)

**Yield: 4 large servings**

*Prep time: 20 minutes*
*Cook time: 45 minutes*
*Total time: 1 hour, 5 minutes*

Traditionally, Tajine Kefta is a meatball dish that's cooked with a tomato base and potatoes, a Moroccan spice mix called ras el hanout, and an egg. It is cooked in a tajine, a cone-shaped lidded pot that you can cook in and eat from. Yamina, one of my closest family friends, tells me that community is the most important part of Moroccan mealtimes. "You cook together, then you eat from the same dish, sitting in a circle and eating with your hands," she adds. "There's something very intimate and special about the experience."

"What exactly is ras el hanout?" I ask Yamina as we're veganizing this recipe. She explains, "Well, *ras el hanout* literally translates to 'head of the spice shop,' and it's similar to a curry mix, meaning that it can be made from many different spice combinations. Traditionally, spice shop owners would create their own mix and sell it as 'ras el hanout.' Nowadays, you can find standardized versions of this spice mix, commonly including ingredients like cardamom, cumin, clove, cinnamon, nutmeg, allspice, ginger, chile peppers, coriander seeds, peppercorns, paprika, fenugreek, and turmeric, at practically any supermarket or specialty store, but I like to enhance some of its flavors, so this recipe is my personal version of Tajine Kefta, and I'd encourage people to be generous with their spices. In Moroccan cuisine, more is more."

To recreate the egg flavor, we've added a little kala namak, or black salt, as its sulfurous flavor is reminiscent of eggs. If you don't have a tajine, just use a large, deep pan with a lid.

*FOR THE SAUCE*

¼ cup (60 mL) olive oil

1 onion, finely chopped

2 garlic cloves, minced

21 ounces (600 g) potatoes, peeled and quartered (about 6 medium potatoes)

1 handful of fresh cilantro, chopped

1 28-ounce (800 g) can crushed tomatoes

2 teaspoons ground cumin

2 teaspoons sweet or smoked paprika

1 teaspoon turmeric powder

½ to 1 teaspoon sea salt, to taste

1 teaspoon ground black pepper

2 tablespoons plus 2 teaspoons ras el hanout (Moroccan spice mix)

2 cups (480 mL) hot water

*FOR THE "MEAT" BALLS*

21 ounces (600 g) vegan minced meat (the raw kind, not the precooked crumbles)

1 onion, finely chopped

1 handful of fresh cilantro, finely chopped

1 teaspoon ground cumin

1 teaspoon sweet or smoked paprika

½ teaspoon ground black pepper

½ teaspoon turmeric powder

½ teaspoon sea salt, or to taste

1 tablespoon plus 1 teaspoon ras el hanout (Moroccan spice mix)

Minced red hot chile pepper, to taste (for those who like very spicy meatballs, optional)

*TO SERVE*

1 pinch of kala namak (black salt; optional)

Moroccan bread, gluten-free if desired, or homemade flatbread (see recipe that follows)

*CONTINUES*

Cultural Food

MAIN DISHES

1. **Start the sauce:** Heat the oil in a tajine or large pot over medium heat. Add the onion and sauté for 3 minutes.

2. Add the garlic and potatoes and cook for another 10 minutes, turning them a few times to brown on all sides.

3. **While the potatoes are cooking, prepare the "meat" balls:** Mix all the ingredients in a large bowl using your hands. Make sure everything is well incorporated. Form about 30 balls (maximum 1 to 1½ inches (2.5 to 3.75 centimeters) in diameter) and set aside.

4. Add the cilantro, crushed tomatoes, cumin, paprika, turmeric, salt and pepper, and ras el hanout to the tajine.

5. Mix the sauce well and add the water. Cook for 10 more minutes, then add the "meat" balls, cover, and let simmer over medium-low heat for 25 minutes (stir occasionally and flip them at least once halfway through).

6. Taste for seasoning and add more salt if needed. Serve with a pinch of kala namak and Moroccan bread, if desired.

 **"1984" by N3rdistan**

# Quick & Easy Homemade Yogurt Flatbread

1 cup (250 g) plain, full-fat, unsweetened vegan yogurt

2¼ cups (280 g) all-purpose flour (gluten-free if desired)

1 pinch of sea salt

½ teaspoon garlic powder (optional)

1. Mix the ingredients in a bowl until you get an even dough.

2. Heat a large nonstick skillet (add 1 teaspoon olive oil if your skillet is not nonstick) over high heat.

3. Separate the dough into 4 balls and either stretch or roll them out until they're thin and oval shaped. Once the skillet is hot, add the flatbreads and cook them for 2 to 3 minutes on each side, until you see golden brown spots.

Yield: 4 flatbreads

*Prep time: 4 minutes*
*Cook time: 4 to 6 minutes*
*Total time: 8 to 10 minutes*

# SRI LANKAN
# PUMPKIN CURRY

## IN MEMORY OF MY FATHER, KNUT C. HANSEN

**In collaboration with**
Iromi Goonasekera Poloni

**Yield: 4 to 6 servings as a side dish**

*Prep time: 15 minutes*
*Cook time: 30 minutes*
*Total time: 45 minutes*

The happiest stories my father used to tell me were always the ones about his time spent in Sri Lanka while in his twenties. His face would light up as he'd describe the nature, the friends he made, the food, and the families who shared their homes with him. One family, he told me, taught him how to make jewelry and how to cook. Our home was filled with spices and handmade jewelry because of it. That family's daughter, Iromi, had become friends with both of my parents while working in Europe. After many years spent abroad (including holidays at my grandparents' house in Belgium), Iromi moved back to Sri Lanka a few decades ago. I reached out to her to ask if she remembered anything in particular about my dad and his favorite recipes. She told me that he loved curries, especially this pumpkin curry, and that he had no issues with the copious amounts of chiles people tend to put in curries in Sri Lanka.

"All vegetable curries are vegan by definition, unless you add some dry fish flakes [Maldive fish], but most people don't do that anymore, mainly because Maldive fish is very expensive!" Iromi explains, adding, "Your father ate with his hands too. I can still see him scooping up curries with a piece of roti or some rice and tucking in. And no matter how spicy, he definitely would have asked to add even more chiles."

- 1 1-pound (500 g) pumpkin, with the skin (see Notes)
- 1 medium onion, finely chopped
- 3 large garlic cloves, minced, or 2 teaspoons garlic paste
- 1 2-inch (5 cm) piece of fresh ginger, grated, or 2 teaspoons ginger paste
- 1 sprig curry leaves (8 to 10 leaves)
- 1 2-inch (5 cm) piece of pandan leaf (see Notes)
- 1 2-inch (5 cm) cinnamon stick
- 1 clove and 1 pod of cardamom, bruised (see Notes)
- 1 or 2 green chiles, split in half (heat is a matter of taste, so the exact amount is up to the cook!)
- 2 teaspoons turmeric powder
- 1 teaspoon sea salt, or to taste
- 1 14-ounce (400 g) can full-fat coconut milk
- ½ to 1 cup (120 to 240 mL) water
- 2 tablespoons cooked white rice (any white rice is fine except parboiled)
- 1 teaspoon cumin seeds
- 10 black peppercorns
- ¼ cup (90 g) freshly grated or desiccated (shredded) coconut
- 1 cup (240 mL) full-fat coconut cream
- 1 dash of lime or lemon juice, or to taste
- Cooked rice or roti, for serving (use rice for a gluten-free option)

 GFO

 INF

Cultural Food

MAIN DISHES

*CONTINUES*

1. Cut the pumpkin into 1-inch (2.5 cm) chunks. Don't remove the skin. If you do, the pumpkin will just disintegrate and become a soup! Place the pieces in a wide, deep pan or pot.

2. Add the onion, garlic, ginger, curry leaves, pandan leaf, cinnamon stick, cardamom, green chiles, turmeric, and salt to the pan.

3. Pour in the coconut milk and water (start with ½ cup/120mL), then add more depending on your desired consistency). The pumpkin should be just submerged.

4. Stir or just shake the pan until everything is settled and bring to a boil over high heat, then lower the heat to medium-low, cover the pan or pot, and let simmer until the pumpkin is tender, about 25 minutes.

5. While the pumpkin is cooking, prepare the remaining condiments: In a small skillet, dry-roast the cooked white rice just until it's pale brown. Don't let it burn or get dark brown. Set aside.

6. Dry-roast the cumin, peppercorns, and coconut for 2 to 3 minutes.

7. Blend the rice, spices, and coconut into a fine paste. A spice grinder is ideal for this, but a standard blender or small food processor will work.

8. Mix the paste with the full-fat coconut cream.

9. By now the pumpkin should be cooked and the coconut milk well reduced. Pour the coconut cream mixture over the cooked pumpkin, but do not stir, or the soft pumpkin will break! Just shake the pan gently. Cook for another 2 to 3 minutes.

10. Taste for seasoning, and add a dash of lime or lemon juice and more salt if needed. Serve with cooked rice or roti.

## NOTES

• A creamy, floury variety of pumpkin is better than the grainy, watery type. The perfect ones for this recipe are pale yellow on the inside, such as kaddu pumpkin. Kabocha squash is a good option too.

• Pandan leaves are fragrant leaves commonly used for flavoring in South Asian and South East Asian cuisines. You can find them in the fresh or frozen sections of Sri Lankan and other Asian markets. If you can't find them, you can simply omit them or use 2 bay leaves instead.

• Iromi's tip: Put the cardamom in a mortar and pound just once or twice to release the aroma.

"American Pie" by Don McLean

"I realized very early the power of food to evoke memory, to bring people together, to transport you to other places—and I wanted to be a part of that."
—CHEF JOSÉ ANDRÉS PUERTA

# INDIAN DAL TADKA

In collaboration with

Nisha Vora, founder of Rainbow Plant Life and cookbook author (India)

Yield: 4 servings

*Prep time: 15 minutes*
*Cook time: 50 minutes*
*Total time: 1 hour, 5 minutes*

For years, Nisha and I lived in the same neighborhood in Brooklyn, New York. Our shared passion for both veganism and food led to many discussions and stories at dinner parties. Even though Nisha grew up in California, she embraces her Indian heritage and continuously finds ways to honor the recipes and traditions her parents taught her.

"Growing up, we ate dal almost every night," Nisha recalls. "My mom always served it alongside *bhat* (rice), *shaak* (any kind of cooked vegetable), and roti (whole-wheat flatbread). She managed to get a nutritious, home-cooked meal on the table every day even though she worked full time. At the time, I didn't appreciate it much, longing for the fast food and pizza dinners my friends ate. It wasn't until I got older and delved into Indian cooking myself that I began to fully understand the gift she was giving us each night. Every family has their own way of making dal, from the type of lentil or pulse used to the types of spices and when they're added. What unites them is that they nourish the mind, soul, and body. The song I chose for this meal is 'Khuda Bhi Aasman' by the American band Khruangbin. It's a cover of a Hindi song from a 1970 Bollywood film that my parents loved when they were growing up. When I first played it for them, they instantly recognized the tune. It's the perfect blending of our Indian and American cultures."

*FOR THE DAL*

1 cup (200 g) yellow mung dal or split red lentils (or a mix of both!)

2 to 3 teaspoons coconut oil or neutral oil of choice (plus more oil if not using a nonstick pan)

1 medium yellow onion, chopped

1 teaspoon sea salt, plus more to taste

4 garlic cloves, minced

1-inch (2.5 cm) piece of fresh ginger, grated or minced (about 1 tablespoon)

1 serrano pepper, diced (deseed for less heat)

1 teaspoon curry powder

¼ teaspoon turmeric powder

1 teaspoon garam masala

2½ to 3½ cups (600 to 840 mL) water (see Notes)

Ground black pepper to taste

1 14.5-ounce (410 g) can diced tomatoes (see Notes)

1 small handful of fresh cilantro, roughly chopped

*FOR THE TADKA*

4½ to 6 teaspoons coconut oil, or neutral oil of choice

1 teaspoon black or brown mustard seeds

½ teaspoon cumin seeds

8 to 10 curry leaves

1 to 2 dried red chile peppers, like Kashmiri peppers (optional)

*TO SERVE*

Fresh cilantro leaves (optional)

White basmati rice or Indian flatbread (choose rice for a gluten-free option)

Vegan coconut yogurt (optional)

Thinly sliced red onion (optional)

GFO

TNF

HP

Cultural Food

MAIN DISHES

*CONTINUES*

1. **Make the dal:** Sort through the lentils and remove any pebbles. Soak the lentils in cold water for 15 minutes, drain, and set aside.

2. Heat the coconut oil in a deep, heavy skillet over medium-high heat. Once the oil is shimmering, add the onion, season with a pinch of salt, and cook for 4 to 5 minutes, until softened.

3. Add the garlic, ginger, and serrano pepper. Cook for 60 to 90 seconds, or until the garlic is lightly browned and the mixture is very fragrant. Add the curry powder, turmeric, and garam masala, stir to coat the onions, and cook for about 30 seconds, stirring almost constantly.

4. Deglaze the pan with the water (I use about 2 cups/480 mL at this stage), scraping up any browned bits on the bottom of the pan. Add the lentils, the 1 teaspoon salt, and black pepper to taste. Stir to combine.

5. Bring the dal to a boil, then lower the heat and partially cover the pan (if your lid has a small hole on top to allow steam to escape, you can fully cover the pan). Simmer the dal for 30 minutes, or until the lentils are fully cooked, stirring occasionally and adding more water as needed to prevent the dal from drying out, about 25 minutes or until the lentils are tender.

6. Add the diced tomatoes and cook for 4 to 5 minutes, until they've cooked down and are basically blended into the dal. (If using fresh tomatoes, cook them until soft and broken down; fresh needs more time than canned). If you want the dal to be thicker/creamier, run an immersion blender through some of the dal, but keep some lentils whole.

7. Stir in the cilantro and remove from the heat.

8. **Make the tadka:** Heat a small frying pan or tempering pan over medium-high heat. Add the coconut oil and, once it's shimmering, add the mustard seeds. When the mustard seeds start popping, add the cumin seeds. After a few seconds, add the curry leaves and dried red chile peppers (if using). Keep stirring or shaking the pan to help cook the spices evenly and prevent burning for 60 to 90 seconds, or until the spices are very aromatic, the curry leaves have shriveled, and the chiles and cumin seeds have darkened. Remove from the heat immediately to prevent overcooking.

9. Pour the tadka over the dal and stir to combine. Taste for seasonings and add salt and pepper as needed. If desired, garnish with additional fresh cilantro. Serve with white rice and coconut yogurt or red onion, if desired.

## NOTES
• *If you want to use fresh tomatoes, use about 1½ cups (300 g) diced.*

• *For a creamy and thick texture, start with 2 cups (480 mL) water and gradually add more throughout the cooking process—about ¾ to 1 cup (180 to 240 mL). If you want a soupier version, start with more than 2 cups (480 mL) water and add more as you go.*

"Khuda Bhi Aasman" by Khruangbin

# HOMEMADE JAPANESE TOFU

In collaboration with

Ko, Kyoko, and
Miko Oyakawa

Yield: 2 large 16- to
20-ounce (450 to 600 g)
tofu pieces

*Prep time: 1 hour*
*Soak time: 7 hours*
*Total time: 8 hours*

"It always felt like a fun and special occasion," Ko, one of my dearest friends, says as he recalls his childhood memories of his family making homemade tofu. He grew up in a Japanese household in Canada but, wanting to reconnect with his parents' culture, he moved to Tokyo on his own when he was just fifteen and has now spent more than half his life there. Tofu is a household staple for most Japanese families, as it's very versatile. It can be used in soups, stews, stir-fries, burgers, salads, sauces, desserts—it can even be eaten on its own or with your topping of choice. One of Ko's favorite dishes is *agedashi dōfu*, a deep-fried tofu served in a light savory broth.

Ko's paternal grandparents immigrated to Canada from the Okinawa islands of Japan in the early 1900s. During World War II, along with thousands of other Japanese Canadians, they were forced into internment camps. Ko's father was born during this time. After the war, in efforts to assimilate their community, the government relocated and scattered the imprisoned Japanese families across rural Canada. In a time when Asian food products were scarce, Japanese families shared recipes, along with other traditional knowledge, to maintain their culture. Ko's mother inherited this knowledge as well.

Some of the major advantages of making homemade tofu are that you can make a lot at once, it's super cost effective, you can adjust the firmness to your liking, and you have the benefits of using the by-products. Soy milk is the obvious one, but the other by-product that often gets overlooked in the West is *okara*, the pulp left over from extracting the soy milk. *Okara* is extremely nutritious and packed with fiber and protein. While it is traditionally eaten as a side dish simmered with vegetables, *unohana*, it can also be used for baking cookies, crackers, muffins, or even making vegan patties and sausages—zero waste!

**2 cups (400 g) dry soybeans**
**2 tablespoons lemon juice (see Notes)**
**½ cup (120 mL) water**

**1.** Soak the beans for approximately 7 hours in 5 cups (1.2 L) water. They will soften and double in size. Once soaked, drain the beans in a strainer.

**2.** Place 1 cup (filling the volume of a 240 mL container) of the soaked beans and 2 cups (480 mL) water in a blender. Blend for 1 minute. Strain the blended mixture through a sieve into a large bowl.

**3.** Repeat this step until all the beans have been blended with water.

GF

TNF

HP

Cultural Food

MAIN DISHES

*CONTINUES*

**4.** Lay a clean cotton cloth (or cheesecloth) over a separate large bowl. Put the blended soybeans into the cloth. Gather up the edges of the cloth to make a bag, lift up the bag, and twist and squeeze out as much liquid as you can. Inside the cotton cloth are the solid leftovers, or okara. (See Notes.)

**5.** Transfer the liquid in the bowl to a large pot and heat over medium heat, stirring occasionally, until the soy liquid comes to a boil. This is now drinkable soy milk.

**6.** Next, to curdle the milk, in a separate measuring cup, mix the lemon juice and the ½ cup (120 mL) water.

**7.** Add the mixture slowly into the hot soy milk. Slowly and gently stir the soy milk to help incorporate the curdling mixture (just 1 or 2 stirs). Let the milk sit for 10 minutes.

**8.** Strain the curdled mixture through a sieve to drain the excess water (this excess water can be used to make soup).

**9.** Lay the cotton cloth over a tofu mold (see Notes) or strainer. Make sure there's another dish underneath to catch the drained liquid. Transfer the curdled mixture onto the cotton cloth.

**10.** Once in the mold, fold the excess cotton cloth over the tofu. Place something flat like a dish on top of the tofu mold. Then set weights, such as canned food or clean rocks, on the surface. Let this sit for 5 to 10 minutes. The longer you wait, the firmer the tofu will get, so adjust the time to your liking.

**11.** Remove the tofu from the cotton cloth. Cut it into large pieces, place in a container, and cover with cold water. The tofu will keep in the cold water in the fridge for about 1 week.

## NOTES

• *To get more soy milk from the okara (step 4), open up the cotton cloth (still over a bowl) and pour about 5 cups (1.2 L) of hot water over the solid okara. Squeeze the cloth again to release all the soy milk.*

• *Tofu mold: You can use many things in place of a traditional tofu mold. Any container with holes at the bottom will work. For example, a bamboo steamer, a hard plastic container, a colander/sieve.*

• *Instead of lemon juice, you could use 1 tablespoon of either nigari or Epsom salts and ½ cup (120 mL) water.*

## SERVING SUGGESTION

**Okinawan Champuru (pictured on page 82).** *Since Ko's family is originally from the Okinawa Islands, he suggested including a serving suggestion for one of Okinawa's most famous dishes:* champuru, *which translates to "something mixed" and is essentially a variation of a stir-fry, often including bitter lemon and/or eggs. For a vegan version, simply sauté and combine bean sprouts, chopped green peppers, chopped chives, shredded Chinese cabbage, chopped scallions, cubed homemade tofu, julienned or grated carrots, white pepper, garlic, saké or mirin, a little soy sauce, salt, and vegan shiitake kombu dashi (broth).*

"Ride on Time" by Priscilla Ahn and "Loop" by SIRUP

# MAORI BOIL-UP

In collaboration with
Daniel Haimona, founder of
Dam Native (Aotearoa/New
Zealand)

Yield: 6 servings
Prep time: 25 minutes
Cook time: 35 minutes
Total time: 1 hour

I lived in Aotearoa (which is the Maori name for New Zealand) from 2003 to 2004 to study visual arts. During my time there, I got to meet some of the most talented and kind people I've ever known, including my friend Daniel Haimona, who taught me about Maori culture, food, and music. This recipe is a vegan twist on a Maori classic, the boil-up. It's a dish Danny's father, the main cook of their *whānau* (a Maori term that both describes and transcends the notion of family, as it includes the nuclear family as well as the extended friends and family circle of a community), used to make for him as a child, especially during the winters. He had learned it from his parents, who used to cook the meat and vegetables in a traditional Maori hangi, a pit dug in the ground and filled with hot rocks to steam food. Later generations then started boiling the ingredients as well.

Maori cuisine is heavily centered on root vegetables, meat, and seafood. Instead of meat, we're using seitan, a protein made from wheat gluten that is very similar to meat in texture. For the smoky flavor, we've added liquid smoke. Traditionally, the only condiments used would be salt and butter, but thanks to Danny's partner, artist Tracey Tawhiao, this version has a few extra ingredients, including some red wine, to add another dimension to the flavor. One of the songs that accompanies this recipe is from Danny's own group, Dam Native, Aotearoa's premier Maori hip-hop group. The boil-up includes kamokamo, a type of squash commonly used in Maori cuisine. It resembles zucchini in color and texture, but it has a round shape.

## FOR THE BOIL-UP

**3 tablespoons olive oil**

**16 to 18 ounces (450 to 500 g) seitan or vegan meat, torn into chunks**

**1 leek, sliced**

**2 celery stalks, chopped**

**1 large onion, chopped**

**4 garlic cloves, minced**

**1 cup (240 mL) red wine**

**4½ cups (1 L plus 80 mL) vegetable broth**

**1½ cups (360 mL) apple juice**

**1 medium sweet potato (known as *kumara* in Aotearoa), peeled and cubed**

**1 medium yellow potato, peeled and cubed (or more sweet potato)**

**2 teaspoons liquid smoke, or more to taste**

**1 teaspoon sea salt, or to taste**

**Pepper to taste**

**2 tablespoons chopped fresh parsley**

**3 to 4 bunches of watercress, stems discarded (or other hearty leafy greens like chard or collard greens)**

## FOR THE KAMOKAMO

**4 cups (500 g) cubed kamokamo (or other type of summer squash like zucchini), with the skin**

**¼ cup (57 g) vegan butter**

**½ cup (120 mL) water**

**Sea salt and ground black pepper to taste**

Cultural Food

MAIN DISHES

*CONTINUES*

1. **For the boil-up:** In a large pot, heat the olive oil over medium-high heat, then add the seitan and brown it for 5 minutes. Add the leek, celery, onion, and garlic and let cook for 5 more minutes before adding the red wine. Stir and cook for another 1 to 2 minutes.

2. Add the vegetable broth and apple juice, bring to a boil, then reduce the heat to low. Add the sweet potato (kumara) and potato, cover the pot with a lid, and simmer for 20 minutes.

3. **Prepare the kamokamo:** While the boil-up simmers, in a separate pot, combine the cubed kamokamo, vegan butter, water, and a little salt and pepper. Cover and let steam over medium heat for 20 to 25 minutes, until the water has evaporated and the kamokamo is tender and slightly caramelized. If using zucchini, this will only take about 10 minutes.

4. Add the liquid smoke, salt and pepper, parsley, and watercress to the pot with the potatoes and let simmer for another 5 to 10 minutes.

5. Either add the kamokamo (or zucchini) to the boil-up or serve it as a side.

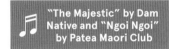
♫ "The Majestic" by Dam Native and "Ngoi Ngoi" by Patea Maori Club

# HAWAIIAN TOFU MUSUBI

### In collaboration with

Marissa Wong, recipe developer and creator of the website It's All Good Vegan

#### Yield: 7 servings

*Prep time: 40 minutes*
*Cook time: 10 minutes*
*Total time: 50 minutes*

Marissa is a longtime Best of Vegan contributor and team member who loves to create a mix of innovative plant-based recipes and veganized versions of her nonvegan favorites. This Hawaiian *musubi* (which translates to "rice ball") is layered with rice and marinated tofu, then wrapped up in nori.

"If you know anything about me," Marissa says, "you know that I grew up in Hawaii, so Spam *musubis* were a popular meal for my family. My mom used to make them for me before hula, when we went to the beach, and pretty much any other activity I can think of. That's what makes these so great. They're quick, easy, and will satisfy any appetite. This has been one of the foods I've missed the most since going vegan, but luckily, not anymore."

> ♫ "Island Style" by John Cruz and "Somewhere Over the Rainbow" by Israel "IZ" Kamakawiwo'ole

**14 ounces (400 g) extra-firm tofu**

**¼ cup (60 mL) gluten-free tamari**

**1 tablespoon sugar**

**4½ teaspoons rice vinegar**

**1 teaspoon onion powder**

**1 garlic clove, minced**

**1 teaspoon avocado oil (or other neutral vegetable oil)**

**3 nori sheets, cut into thirds**

**1 cup (200 g) cooked white sushi rice, cooled completely**

**1.** Press the tofu using a tofu press or by placing it between layers of paper towels, adding extra weight (like a heavy book) to remove excess water. Cut the pressed tofu into 7 even rectangular slabs.

**2.** Combine the tamari and sugar in a small pot and mix. Heat for 2 minutes or until the sugar has dissolved. Immediately take off the heat.

**3.** Pour the tamari and sugar mixture into a large baking dish. Add the rice vinegar, onion powder, and garlic and whisk. Place the tofu in the dish, spaced evenly, and marinate in the refrigerator for 10 minutes. Flip the tofu and marinate for an additional 10 minutes.

**4.** Heat a large nonstick pan over medium heat and add the oil and tofu. Fry on both sides for 3 minutes or until golden brown. For a more flavorful tofu, pour the leftover marinade on the tofu while frying. The sauce will thicken and caramelize.

**5.** To assemble the tofu musubi I use a musubi maker press. Lay one piece of nori horizontally, shiny side down, on a work surface.

**6.** Place the musubi mold in the middle of the nori vertically. Put ⅓ cup (66 g) cooked rice evenly in the mold. Press the rice down using the flat part of the mold, making an even pressed layer of rice. Don't be afraid to really press down, as this will ensure the rice stays together. If you don't have a musubi maker press, simply use your hands to shape the rice. It's sticky, so this will be easy to do. Use the size of the tofu as guidance.

**7.** Place the fried tofu on top of the rice and remove the musubi mold.

**8.** Wrap the nori around the rice and tofu. The nori should stick together, but if it doesn't you can add a drop of water at the ends to seal it.

**9.** Repeat until you have assembled all your musubis.

### NOTE

*To add more flavor, sprinkle some nori komi furikake (rice seasoning) on top of your rice. Just make sure it does not have dried fish flakes in it to keep it vegan.*

 GF
 TNF
 HP

Cultural Food

**MAIN DISHES**

# PANAMANIAN
# TAMAL DE OLLA

### In collaboration with
### Nina Herrera (Panamá)

### Yield: 5 to 6 servings
*Prep time: 30 minutes*
*Cook time: 1 hour, 20 minutes*
*Total time: 1 hour, 50 minutes*

Tamal de Olla is a Panamanian specialty similar to tamales, but cooked in a pan (*olla* means "pan") and omitting the banana leaves. My friend Nina, a chef and previously a restaurant owner, whom I met in New York several years ago, tells me that when she was little, she and her family would drive for several hours to visit their extended family in the countryside, far from Panamá City. The traditional recipe for Tamal de Olla includes shredded chicken, which often came from the local farms or family members' backyard chicken coops.

"I didn't make the connection at the time," says Nina, "but now that I'm vegan, I'm glad I'm able to enjoy a chicken-less version of this dish." Marinated soy curls, creamy polenta, and a tomato-vegetable base with fried capers give this recipe its depth of flavor and creamy texture.

*FOR THE SOY CURLS*
5.25 ounces (150 g) large soy curls/textured vegetable protein (not the small granules, but those sometimes labeled "chicken style," those from the Butler brand are ideal)

1 tablespoon dried oregano

1½ teaspoons sea salt

½ teaspoon ground black pepper

4 cups (1 L) boiling water

*FOR THE CREAMY CORN*
3 cups (720 mL) water

1½ cups (210 g) cornmeal or cornflour (also called corn maize, it is yellow in color and is not the same as cornstarch)

1 to 2 cups (240 to 480 mL) vegetable broth

¼ cup (57 g) vegan butter

Sea salt to taste

*FOR THE TAMAL BASE*
2 tablespoons olive oil

2 teaspoons achiote seeds

1 red chile pepper, finely sliced

1 onion, diced

1 red bell pepper, diced

4 garlic cloves, minced

Sea salt and pepper to taste

½ cup (120 mL) red wine

2 tablespoons gluten-free tamari or soy sauce

1 tablespoon red wine vinegar

1 teaspoon dried oregano

2 large tomatoes, chopped

1 14-ounce (400 mL) can tomato puree (passata)

3 to 4 tablespoons pitted green olives, sliced

3 to 4 tablespoons raisins

*FOR THE FRIED CAPERS*
2 teaspoons olive oil

3 tablespoons capers

**1.** **Make the soy curls:** Place the soy curls, oregano, salt, and pepper in a large bowl. Pour the boiling water over the soy curls and spices and mix well. Cover with a lid or plate and let soak for at least 15 to 20 minutes.

**2.** Drain the soy curls and set aside.

**3.** **Make the creamy corn:** In a large pot, bring the water to a boil.

**4.** Slowly add the cornmeal (to avoid clumping), and cook for 3 to 5 minutes over medium-high heat.

**5.** Reduce the heat to medium-low, cover, and simmer for 15 minutes, occasionally stirring and adding vegetable broth as needed, making sure the texture is creamy and thick, and not runny.

**6.** When the creamy corn is fully cooked, mix in the vegan butter and set aside.

**MAIN DISHES** | **Cultural Food**

*CONTINUES*

**7. Make the *tamal* base:** When you start the water boiling for the creamy corn, combine the olive oil and achiote in a large nonstick pan. Cook over medium heat for 2 to 3 minutes, then remove the achiote (it's meant to add flavor and color to the oil).

**8.** Add the drained soy curls, red chile pepper, onion, bell pepper, garlic, and a pinch each of salt and pepper. Sauté over medium heat for 10 minutes, then slowly add the red wine, tamari, red wine vinegar, and oregano. Cook for another 5 minutes.

**9.** Add the chopped tomatoes and tomato puree, cover, reduce the heat to low, and simmer for 25 minutes. Remove about ¾ cup (180 mL) of the tomato base (but none of the soy curls) and blend it into the creamy corn layer using an immersion blender. The corn layer's consistency should be thick and creamy, a bit like that of firm mashed potatoes.

**10. Fry the capers:** Heat the olive oil in a small skillet over high heat. Once hot, add the capers and fry for 2 to 3 minutes until crispy, then remove from the heat.

**11. Assemble and bake the *tamal*:** Preheat the oven to 350°F (180°C). Add the green olives, raisins, and fried capers to the soy curl mixture. Let simmer for another 5 minutes.

**12.** Finally, transfer the tamal base to a deep ovenproof dish (about 8 x 10 inches/20 x 25 cm) and top with the creamy corn layer. Bake for 15 minutes.

"Panamá Gris" by Pash, feat. Ramses Perez

# CHILES EN NOGADA

## (Mexican Filled Peppers)

### IN MEMORY OF MARIA "CANDE" CANDELARIA

In collaboration with chef and author Neto from Neto Craves

Yield: 4 servings

*Prep time: 30 minutes*
*Cook time: 1 hour*
*Total time: 1 hour, 30 minutes*

This recipe is a twist on traditional Chiles en Nogada, which are normally made with a walnut-based sauce; my friend Neto's grandmother's recipe served as inspiration. Neto and I met only a few weeks after we both started our vegan food Instagram accounts and, after realizing that our birthdays were only a day apart, soon discovered how much else we had in common. He's known for his fast-paced recipe videos that are often vegan renditions of Mexican classics. For this version of Chiles en Nogada, we use a silken tofu- or cashew-based cream and a filling made with hearty ingredients like squash, mushrooms, carrots, and potatoes.

"When I think about Chiles en Nogada," Neto recalls, "it takes me back to my grandma's house, where she used to cook them for the entire family. The whole house smelled like spices. It was so spicy that everyone was coughing. She would be making homemade tortillas and she was always playing music in the background, songs by Juan Gabriel, La Sonora Dinamita, and Selena. This recipe is a spin on her original. She was a great chef, and we would all just hang out at her place, usually at least twenty of us, because everyone knew how good she was. She used to make everything from scratch and the kitchen was always so foggy, with ten pots cooking at the same time, and the whole family in the kitchen talking to her. When I think of a strong Mexican woman, I think of my grandma. She was such a beautiful person, such a light. I miss her a lot, but it brings me so much happiness to be able to make her recipes and turn them vegan. I want to keep that tradition alive."

4 to 8 poblano peppers (poblano peppers can vary in size, so use either 4 larger or 8 smaller peppers)

2 tablespoons olive oil, plus more if needed

1 cup (135 g) diced potatoes (like Yukon Golds, peeled or not, depending on preference)

1 large summer squash or zucchini, diced, about 3½ cups (400 g)

1 large carrot, diced

2 cups (200 g) mushrooms, chopped, or *huitlacoche* (corn smut)

1 small white onion, chopped

1 red bell pepper, chopped

½ cup (60 g) pecans, chopped (optional)

Juice of 2 limes (about 4 tablespoons)

½ teaspoon ground cumin

½ teaspoon paprika

1 teaspoon minced garlic

Sea salt and ground black pepper to taste

½ cup (85 g) pomegranate seeds

Fresh cilantro

*FOR THE CREMA*

1 cup (140 g) cashews (preferably soaked for at least 4 to 6 hours and drained) or 10.5 ounces (300 g) silken tofu

½ cup (120 mL) water or unsweetened plant milk (for cashews, or ¼ cup (60 mL) for silken tofu)

Juice of 1 lemon (2 tablespoons)

1 teaspoon onion powder

Sea salt and pepper to taste

1 pinch of dried oregano, dried basil, or garlic powder (optional)

*CONTINUES*

GF

Cultural Food

**MAIN DISHES**

1. Preheat the oven to 425°F (220°C) and place the whole poblano peppers on a baking tray. Bake for 25 to 30 minutes, flipping them halfway through, until they start turning black. When the poblanos are ready, place them in an airtight glass container, seal, and allow the peppers to steam as they cool. Wrapping them in paper towels also works.

2. While the peppers cool, heat the olive oil in a large skillet and add the potatoes. Sauté over medium heat until they are just halfway cooked, about 8 minutes. The potatoes should still be firm. Then add the squash, carrot, mushrooms, onion, bell pepper, pecans (if using), lime juice, cumin, paprika, garlic, and salt and pepper and sauté over medium-low heat for 10 to 15 minutes, adding a little more olive oil if need be, until the vegetables are tender but still crispy. Set aside.

3. Once the poblanos are cool, remove the skins. Carefully cut a slit along the long side of each pepper. No need to remove the seeds as they are edible. Stuff the peppers with your cooked veggie filling. Reheat them in the oven for a few minutes. You may also add some vegan cheese and bake until the cheese is fully melted (this is optional).

4. Put all the crema ingredients in a blender and blend until completely smooth. Before serving, heat the crema in a saucepan for a few minutes.

5. Pour the warm crema on top of the stuffed poblanos and sprinkle with pomegranate seeds and fresh cilantro.

"Que Nadie Sepa Mi Sufrir" by La Sonora Dinamita

# FILLED CABBAGE ROLLS

Yield: 4 servings (8 cabbage rolls)

*Prep time: 30 minutes*
*Cook time: 1 hour, 10 minutes*
*Total time: 1 hour, 40 minutes*

My paternal grandmother was part of the East Prussian Mennonites whose ancestors had emigrated from the region of Friesland in the Netherlands because of religious persecution. During World War II, when she was just a teenager, they were once again forced to leave and find a new home. She ended up living near the Danish-German border, which is where my father was born. Her Mennonite roots were always mysterious to me, with only pictures and stories reminding us that she'd once had a completely different life. This recipe is a tribute to her, as it is common in Mennonite communities as well as in quite a few Eastern European countries, making it a nostalgic dish for many.

GF

TNF

HP

Cultural Food

♫ "Grandma's Hands" by Bill Withers

## FOR THE ROLLS

8 medium to large savoy cabbage leaves, or other cabbage with soft leaves such as napa cabbage (see Notes)

2 tablespoons olive oil or vegan butter

1 medium to large yellow or white onion, finely chopped

4 garlic cloves, minced

21 ounces (600 g) vegan mince (raw beef style, not crumbles)

1 cup (200 g) cooked brown rice (see Notes)

¾ teaspoon sea salt

½ teaspoon ground black pepper

1 tablespoon chopped fresh parsley, for garnish

Cracked black pepper, for garnish

## OPTIONAL ADD-ONS (see Notes)

1 teaspoon paprika

½ teaspoon ground cumin

1 teaspoon liquid smoke

¼ to ½ teaspoon kala namak (black salt)

## FOR THE SAUCE

1 14-ounce (400 g) can crushed tomatoes

1 cup (240 mL) tomato puree (passata)

2 tablespoons coconut sugar or maple syrup

½ teaspoon sea salt, or to taste

1 teaspoon vegetable broth powder (optional)

1. The cabbage needs to be softened before you roll it up. You can achieve this either by steaming it for a few minutes, or by placing it in the freezer a few hours before making this recipe and then letting it thaw for 30 to 60 minutes.

2. Preheat the oven to 350°F (180°C).

3. In a medium skillet, warm the olive oil over medium heat, add the onion and garlic and sauté for 5 minutes, until softened and just beginning to color. Set aside.

4. In a large bowl, combine the vegan mince, cooked rice, salt, pepper, parsley, any add-ons you want, and the sautéed onion and garlic; mix using a wooden spoon, a spatula, or your hands.

5. Fill each cabbage leaf with ⅓ to ½ cup of the filling, then roll them up and place them seam side down in a deep baking dish just large enough to hold them snugly.

6. Make the sauce by mixing all the sauce ingredients in a bowl, then pour it over the cabbage rolls.

7. Cover the baking dish with an ovenproof lid or aluminum foil. Bake for 1 hour and 15 minutes.

8. Garnish with a little cracked pepper and fresh parsley and serve.

## NOTES

• *If you'd like to use up a whole cabbage head, you can simply make more smaller rolls, using less filling per roll.*

• *If you don't have precooked rice, cook slightly more than ⅓ cup (65 g) dry rice according to the package instructions to obtain 1 cup (200 g) of cooked rice.*

• *Traditionally, cabbage rolls are made with very few spices. The suggested add-ons will enhance the flavor, but just know that they wouldn't normally be added.*

# GREEK PITA WITH TZATZIKI

### In collaboration with
Eleni McMullin, photographer, recipe developer, and content creator (Convey the Moment, The Kindest Plate)

### Yield: 2 servings
*Prep time: 10 minutes*
*Cook time: 10 to 15 minutes*
*Total time: 20 to 25 minutes*

Eleni is a Greek-Canadian vegan fashion and food blogger I've known for many years. Her recipes are always popular when we feature them on Best of Vegan, and this Greek Pita with Tzatziki is one of the most popular recipes we've ever shared on the platform. And for a good reason: It's simple to make, high in protein, packed with flavor, and a guaranteed crowd-pleaser. The tzatziki sauce alone is worth giving it a try! It's also a recipe that is closely linked to Eleni's memories of her family in Greece and all her trips back home when she was little. "It's so special to keep the tradition alive with my own family now too," she says. "I love sharing old traditional foods with my kids and showing them how easily they can be made vegan."

*FOR THE ROASTED CHICKPEAS*
1 14-ounce (400 g) can no-sodium chickpeas, drained and rinsed
Juice of 1 lemon (2 tablespoons)
1 teaspoon olive oil
1 pinch of oregano
1 pinch of sea salt
1 pinch of ground black pepper

*FOR THE TZATZIKI*
1 cup (240 mL) vegan mayonnaise
Juice of ½ lemon (1 tablespoon)
1 tablespoon red wine vinegar
2 tablespoons shredded cucumber
2 garlic cloves, minced (preferably pressed through a garlic press)
1 teaspoon olive oil
1 pinch of ground black pepper
1 tablespoon chopped fresh dill, or more to taste

*FOR THE WRAPS*
Red onion
Fresh tomatoes
Lettuce
2 pita breads, gluten-free if desired

**1. Prepare the chickpeas:** Preheat the oven to 350°F (180°C). Line a baking tray with parchment paper.

**2.** In a small bowl, mix the chickpeas with the lemon juice and olive oil. Add the oregano, salt, and pepper, then spread over the lined baking tray.

**3.** Bake for 10 to 15 minutes, until the chickpeas are crispy and toasty brown.

**4. While the chickpeas are baking, mix all the ingredients for the tzatziki.** Place in the fridge to keep cool while you chop your veggies.

**5.** Chop the onion, tomatoes, and lettuce for the wraps. Use as much or as little as you want.

**6.** In a small frying pan over medium heat, warm the pita breads to soften them.

**7.** Once the chickpeas are cooked, combine everything in the pita and enjoy.

"Seven Days in Sunny June" by Jamiroquai

GFO

TNF

HP

Cultural Food

MAIN DISHES

# KOREAN TTEOKBOKKI
## TWO WAYS

In collaboration with

Joanne Lee Molinaro
("The Korean Vegan"),
*New York Times*
bestselling author

I met Joanne, aka the Korean Vegan, in 2017 when she was a full-time lawyer who had started a Korean vegan food blog on the side. She wanted to document her newfound vegan lifestyle and create a platform to share her favorite Korean recipes, but also to provide an outlet to write about her life. Joanne is now a full-time creator who's taken the TikTok and Instagram worlds by storm with her videos that combine mouthwatering recipes with deeply personal, vulnerable, and inspiring messages. Her debut cookbook, *The Korean Vegan Cookbook*, is a *New York Times* bestseller.

I was immediately drawn to Joanne's beautiful cooking videos and mesmerizing captions. We soon met in person and became friends. She'd often come visit me and other friends in New York City, and during those trips she'd cook many delicious Korean dishes, including these two versions of *tteokbokki*, introducing me to the magic of gochujang and rice cakes.

We'd also spend hours talking about family and identity, among other things. Specifically, about how lost she felt growing up as a Korean child in Illinois. "When I was in public and I was at school, I was American, I spoke English, perfect English," Joanne told me once. "I wore all the same clothes that my American friends were wearing. I tried to fit in as much as I could. But then when I was at home, we only spoke Korean and we only ate Korean food. We had very strict rules at my house about studying and homework and television, and even friends and things like that. I was not happy about being Korean for a very long time when I was younger, because when you're little, you just want to fit in with everyone else. I felt so much on the outside, I had black hair, not blond hair. I had this yellow skin, not white skin. I wanted to be like everyone else. I didn't want to associate with being Korean, I wanted to be American, American, American, American. I was bringing the wrong food with me to lunch sometimes. There were just too many things that were different, and I really was ashamed of that. Now, my mom tells me, 'Look at how much kimchi you're eating. When you were little, you would always tell me, "Mommy, I'm not Korean, I'm American," and now look at you, you're more Korean than I am.'"

In Joanne Lee Molinaro's own words, here are two versions of one of her favorite dishes: *tteokbokki*.

Cultural Food

MAIN DISHES

*CONTINUES*

# Spicy Tteokbokki
떡볶이

Spicy *tteokbokki* is very popular in Korea. It is a bar/street food item. It's very spicy and it's made with gochujang, a Korean red chili paste, and *gochugaru*, Korean chili powder, as well as a sweetener like sugar. The main ingredient is the rice cake, which is called *garaetteok*. *Garaetteok* is basically steamed rice made from a very specific kind of rice flour, meaning that you can't just take rice and mash it up; that wouldn't work. The *garaetteok* is shaped into these long tubes. This spicy version is what very busy, tired professionals will eat on their way home from work. There are a lot of contests in Korea to see who can eat the spiciest *tteokbokki*. I remember when I was ten years old, I went to a *tteokbokki* house right by my aunt's house, and it was so incredibly spicy. *Tteokbokki* can have all sorts of added ingredients. I've seen it with ramen noodles (which, together, is called *rabokki*), hard-boiled eggs, fried dumplings. *Tteok* means "rice cake" and *bokki* means "something fried."

21 ounces (600 g) tube-shaped garaetteok (rice cakes)

1 tablespoon sesame oil

1 teaspoon cracked black pepper

1 tablespoon olive oil

4 scallions (both white and green parts), chopped

¼ cup (15 g) julienned onion

3 garlic cloves, minced

2 tablespoons gochugaru

¼ cup (60 mL) gluten-free gochujang

2 tablespoons maple syrup

1 tablespoon soy sauce (or tamari for a gluten-free version)

2 cups (480 mL) water

1 tablespoon toasted sesame seeds

**1.** Place the garaetteok in a large bowl. Add the sesame oil and black pepper and stir so that the rice cakes are evenly coated. Set aside.

**2.** Heat the olive oil in a large pan over medium-high heat. When the oil is hot and shimmery, add the scallions, onion, and garlic. Cook until fragrant, about 3 minutes.

**3.** Add the rice cakes, together with the gochugaru, gochujang, and maple syrup. Stir until the rice cakes are evenly coated.

**4.** Deglaze the pan with the soy sauce and then add water. Bring the broth to a boil, then lower the heat to medium-low. Cook until the rice cakes are tender and the broth reduces to a thick sauce, 5 to 10 minutes.

**5.** Garnish with toasted sesame seeds.

Yield: 4 servings
*Prep time: 10 minutes*
*Cook time: 15 minutes*
*Total time: 25 minutes*

# Soy Sauce Tteokbokki

## 궁중떡볶이

### A VARIATION OF GUNGJUNG TTEOKBOKKI

The second version I wanted to share is the *gungjung tteokbokki*, or royal/palatial *tteokbokki*, which would traditionally be served in the royal palace. My mom just calls it "soy sauce *tteokbokki*" because the thing that makes it palatial or royal is the marinated and grilled meat. Since there is no meat in this one, it's easier to just call it "soy sauce *tteokbokki*." I prefer this version because I love soy sauce so much. My mom makes this for me a lot, almost every time I go to her house. She makes her traditional recipe, but just leaves out the meat. It tastes phenomenal, especially if you add some shiitake mushrooms to give it the earthiness it would normally get from meat.

21 ounces (600 g) tube-shaped garaetteok (rice cakes)

4 shiitake mushrooms, sliced

1 tablespoon sesame oil

3 tablespoons soy sauce (or tamari for a gluten-free version)

1 teaspoon cracked black pepper

1 tablespoon olive oil

2 scallions (both white and green parts), chopped

¼ cup (15 g) julienned onion

3 cloves garlic, minced

¼ cup (40 g) julienned green bell pepper

¼ cup (40 g) julienned red bell pepper

1 carrot, sliced into ¼-inch (0.65 cm) discs

2 tablespoons maple syrup

2 cups (480 mL) water

1 tablespoon toasted sesame seeds

**1.** Place the garaetteok and mushrooms in a large bowl. Add the sesame oil, 1 tablespoon of the soy sauce, and the black pepper and stir so that the rice cakes are evenly coated. Set aside.

**2.** Heat the olive oil in a large pan over medium-high heat. When the oil is hot and shimmery, add the scallions, onion, and garlic. Cook until fragrant, about 3 minutes.

**3.** Add the green and red bell peppers and carrot, and continue cooking until the vegetables begin to soften, about 2 minutes.

**4.** Add the rice cakes and mushrooms, together with the remaining 2 tablespoons tamari and the maple syrup. Stir until the rice cakes are evenly coated.

**5.** Add the water, bring the broth to a boil, and then lower the heat to medium-low. Cook until the rice cakes are tender and the broth reduces to a thick sauce, 5 to 10 minutes.

**6.** Garnish with toasted sesame seeds.

Yield: 4 servings

*Prep time: 10 minutes*
*Cook time: 15 minutes*
*Total time: 25 minutes*

"Beautiful Farewell
(아름다운 이별)"
by Kim Gun Mo (김건모)

MAIN DISHES

# CUBAN ROPA VIEJA

**In collaboration with**
Samantha Bailey, plant-based nutrition counselor

**Yield: 4 servings**
*Prep time: 20 minutes*
*Cook time: 30 minutes*
*Total time: 50 minutes*

Samantha, one of Best of Vegan's senior editors (if you follow @bestofvegan on Instagram, you'll likely have seen her in many of our videos) and a nutrition counselor, is of Jamaican and Cuban descent. During one of her trips to Cuba to visit family, she learned how to make Ropa Vieja, which translates to "old clothes," Cuba's signature dish. According to one of the many legends that exist about its origin, a poor old man in Spain who had nothing left to feed his family decided to gather all his old clothes, tear them into shreds, and cook them. A saint appeared to him and performed a miracle, turning the old man's clothes into meat shreds, Ropa Vieja. The recipe then traveled from Europe to Central and South America, and it is now a popular dish in many countries, including Panamá, Puerto Rico, Venezuela, and Columbia, but most of all, Cuba.

Samantha and I veganized this recipe together using young jackfruit to mimic the look and texture of the original dish's shredded meat.

> ♫ "Quimbara" by Celia Cruz, Johnny Pacheco, and Willie Colón and "El Cuarto de Tula" by Buena Vista Social Club

2 14-ounce (400 g) cans young jackfruit (in brine or water, not syrup) or king oyster mushrooms, see Note

2 tablespoons olive oil

1 onion, thinly sliced

2 teaspoons liquid smoke

2 teaspoons tamari (or soy sauce if not gluten-free)

6 garlic cloves, minced

½ green bell pepper, diced

½ red bell pepper, diced

1 red chile pepper, chopped

2 teaspoons ground cumin

½ teaspoon smoked paprika

1 teaspoon dried oregano

1 teaspoon dried thyme

½ teaspoon sea salt, or to taste

Ground black pepper to taste

2 dried bay leaves

½ cup (120 mL) dry white wine

½ cup (120 mL) vegetable broth

2 tablespoons chopped fresh parsley

3 tablespoons sliced green olives

½ cup (120 mL) tomato puree (passata)

*TO SERVE*
2 cups (350 g) cooked black beans, lightly seasoned

2 cups (400 g) cooked white rice

2 sliced and fried ripe plantains (see Congolese "Chicken" Moambé on page 71)

Cilantro (optional)

**1.** Rinse and drain the jackfruit, then remove any hard pieces or cores and tear the remaining parts into shreds. Set aside.

**2.** Heat the oil in a large nonstick pan, add the onion, and sauté over medium heat for 5 minutes. Add the jackfruit and sauté for 5 more minutes.

**3.** Add the liquid smoke, tamari, garlic, bell peppers, chile pepper, cumin, paprika, oregano, thyme, salt, and pepper, and mix.

**4.** Sauté for 5 more minutes, then add the bay leaves and white wine and stir. Reduce the heat to medium-low, cover, and let simmer for 10 minutes.

**5.** Add the broth, parsley, olives, and tomato puree and cook for another 5 minutes.

**6.** Remove the bay leaves and serve with the black beans, rice, and fried plantains.

## NOTE

*If you can't find jackfruit, you can shred king oyster mushrooms using a vegetable peeler. A mix of both jackfruit and king oyster mushrooms works as well!*

GF

TNF

HP

Cultural Food

MAIN DISHES

# JAMAICAN ACKEE & FRIED DUMPLINGS

### In collaboration with
Lloyd Rose, creator of Plant Crazii, chef, and cookbook author

### Ackee: 4 servings
*Prep time: 10 minutes*
*Cook time: 15 minutes*
*Total time: 25 minutes*

### Fried Dumplings: 4 servings
*Prep time: 10 minutes*
*Cook time: 10 minutes*
*Total time: 20 minutes*

Lloyd is one of Best of Vegan's Montréal-based contributors, and the following two recipes honor his roots as a Canadian-Jamaican who, in a quest to navigate the in-betweenness, learned to embrace both of his cultures. In Lloyd's words, "Eating Jamaican food at home and Canadian food outside has been what I've lived for the big majority of my life. Although I grew up in Montréal, Canada, my Jamaican mother made sure we maintained our roots inside the house."

This first recipe, Ackee, is a very popular traditional Jamaican dish that is usually served with saltfish, or seaweed when made by the vegetarian Rastafari community. Ackee, for those who are not familiar with it, is a fruit that is very tender and almost resembles scrambled eggs in look and texture. This recipe can be enjoyed for breakfast or lunch.

*FOR THE ACKEE*
**1 19-ounce (540 g) can ackee**

**1 onion, diced**

**⅓ red bell pepper**

**⅓ yellow bell pepper**

**⅓ green bell pepper**

**1 medium tomato**

**½ Scotch bonnet pepper, seeds removed and minced (optional, as it's very spicy! Be sure to wash your hands thoroughly to avoid burns.)**

**2 tablespoons neutral vegetable oil, like sunflower or canola oil, but not coconut oil**

**1½ teaspoons all-purpose seasoning**

**Sea salt and pepper to taste**

*FOR THE FRIED DUMPLINGS*
**2 cups (250 g) all-purpose flour**

**1 teaspoon baking powder**

**1 teaspoon sea salt**

**1½ teaspoons brown sugar**

**1 tablespoon vegan butter**

**½ cup (120 mL) water, at room temperature**

**High-heat neutral vegetable oil for frying**

**1. Make the ackee:** Empty the cans of ackee into a strainer, rinse gently, and set aside.

**2.** Prepare the vegetables by julienning or slicing the onion, bell peppers, and tomato.

**3.** In a large nonstick skillet, bring the oil to medium heat and sauté the scotch bonnet pepper, onion, and bell peppers until the onion becomes translucent, about 5 minutes. Then gently add in the ackee, tomatoes, and salt and pepper to taste.

**4.** Gently mix everything together using a spatula, being careful to not mash or break the ackee pieces. Then simmer over medium-low heat for 5 to 7 minutes. If you're not using a nonstick pan, you may need to use a little more oil and add a few tablespoons of water. Set aside.

**5. Meanwhile, make the fried dumplings:** Combine the flour, baking powder, salt, and brown sugar in a bowl and mix everything together using your hands.

**6.** Crumble the butter into the flour mix until there are no chunks left.

**7.** Add the water a little at a time (you may not need the entire ½ cup/120 mL). You want just enough to create a dough that can be shaped into a big ball without breaking apart. The dough should be on the drier side and not stick to your fingers. Then form about 8 balls.

**8.** In a deep pot, heat about 2 inches (5 cm) of vegetable oil over medium-high heat to 350°F (180°C).

**9.** Deep-fry the dumplings in the oil until golden brown on each side, about 4 to 6 minutes total. Drain on paper towels to remove excess oil.

**10.** Serve the ackee with the warm fried dumplings on the side.

"Skankin' Sweet" by Chronixx

# MONTRÉAL-STYLE POUTINE

In collaboration with
Lloyd Rose, creator of Plant Crazii, chef, and cookbook author

Yield: 4 to 6 servings
(as an appetizer or side dish)

*Prep time: 30 minutes*
*Cook time: 20 minutes*
*Total time: 50 minutes*

Poutine has been a popular dish in Canada's French-speaking province, Quebec, since the 1950s. It's a comforting combination of French fries, gravy, and cheese. This is the kind of dish that Lloyd, a regular contributor at Best of Vegan, would eat outside of his Jamaican home while growing up in Montréal, Canada. I have family in Montréal as well and so whenever I go to visit, I love ordering a poutine at one of the city's many vegan restaurants.

♫ "Mood" by WizKid, feat. Buju

### FOR THE BROWN GRAVY

3 tablespoons vegan butter

3 tablespoons all-purpose flour, gluten-free if desired

2 cups (480 mL) vegetable broth

3 tablespoons low-salt gluten-free tamari or soy sauce

¼ teaspoon onion powder

¼ teaspoon garlic powder

¼ teaspoon ground black pepper

Sea salt to taste

### FOR THE FRIES

2 pounds (1 kg) russet potatoes (see Note)

High-heat neutral vegetable oil for deep frying

1½ cups (200 g) torn chunks of vegan mozzarella cheese or any white vegan cheese you can find (not shreds!), for topping (the Mozzarella-Style Pizza Cheese on page 207 is ideal)

1. **Make the gravy:** In a medium saucepan, melt the butter over medium-low heat, then mix in the flour until it has dissolved into the butter. There should be no clumps.

2. Gently stir in the vegetable broth and tamari until everything is combined. Bring this mixture to a light boil over medium heat.

3. Mix in the onion powder, garlic powder, and black pepper; taste and add salt if needed.

4. **Make the fries:** Peel the russet potatoes well, then cut them into ½-inch (1.25 cm) sticks.

5. Place the potato sticks in a large bowl and rinse them well in cold water to remove the starch. You will know they are well rinsed once the water is no longer cloudy and becomes clear. Pat them dry to prepare for frying.

6. Fill a deep pot with 3 to 4 inches (7.5 to 10 cm) of oil and heat it to 300°F (150°C). Deep-fry the potato sticks for 7 minutes, then remove them from the oil and drain on paper towels for 10 minutes to allow the heat to distribute evenly throughout the sticks. Then return them to the oil and cook for 3 to 4 more minutes, or until the exterior is golden brown.

7. Remove the fries from the oil and place them on paper towels to absorb the excess oil.

8. **Assemble the poutine:** Place the fries in a large serving bowl, scatter the cheese on top of the fries, and pour just enough brown gravy over them to coat the entire top of your poutine.

9. Eat away and continue to add gravy as you descend from layer to layer into your poutine.

### NOTE

*You can also use frozen, ready-made fries, in which case you can skip step 5.*

GFO

Cultural Food

**MAIN DISHES**

# KURDISH
# APRAX/DOLMA

## Tangy Stuffed Vegetables with Herbed Aromatic Rice

In collaboration with

Seiran Sinjari, recipe developer and creator of Salt & Tahini (Kurdistan and Sweden)

Yield: 6 servings

*Prep time: 35 minutes*
*Cook time: 1 hour, 35 minutes*
*Total time: 2 hours, 10 minutes*

**GF**

**TNF**

**HP**

**Cultural Food**

**MAIN DISHES**

Seiran is a Stockholm-based Best of Vegan contributor and the author of the bestofvegan.com recipe column "All About the Veg." Just like Lloyd, the collaborator on the previous two recipes, Seiran grew up between two cultures: her parents' Kurdish culture and the Swedish culture she was born into. The next two recipes therefore honor both of them.

The first recipe is for *aprax*, or dolma, as they're more widely known. "They fill the house with an irresistible scent of fresh herbs, aromatics, and tangy lemons—a scent that throws me right back to my childhood."

*Aprax* are made across all of Kurdistan and many other parts of the Middle East and the Mediterranean area. For her vegan Kurdish *aprax* filling, Seiran uses rice, brown lentils, and fresh herbs as the base. "What's typical for the Kurdish version is that we often combine different kinds of vegetables and we use a lot of fresh herbs," she explains. "Dill is a must." Seiran, whose name is derived from *seyran*, adds, "*Seyran* in Kurdish means a spring outing in beautiful nature with lots of food, often including *aprax*."

### FOR THE VEGGIES TO STUFF

1 1.8-ounce (50 g) package sun-dried spicy peppers (or 3 or 4 small bell peppers)

3 or 4 baby zucchini

2 medium eggplant

Half of a 23-ounce (650 g) jar preserved grape leaves

2 large red onions

2 large white onions

### FOR THE FILLING

1⅓ cups (250 g) short-grain white rice, rinsed and drained

1 cup (200 g) cooked brown lentils (see Notes)

1 medium bunch of fresh dill, finely chopped

1 medium bunch of fresh parsley, finely chopped

⅓ medium leek, white part only, finely chopped

4 garlic cloves, minced

4½ teaspoons seven-spice blend (baharat)

2 teaspoons Aleppo chile powder or 1 teaspoon red pepper flakes

½ teaspoon ground cumin

¼ cup (60 mL) tomato paste

⅓ cup plus 1 tablespoon (95 mL) olive oil

Juice of 2 lemons (about ¼ cup/60 mL)

3 to 4 tablespoons pomegranate molasses, depending on how sour your molasses is (see Notes)

1 tablespoon sea salt, or to taste (generally you need to season well with salt to balance the acidity)

Ground black pepper to taste

### FOR THE BOTTOM OF THE PAN (YOU CAN USE A COMBINATION OF ALL OR JUST POTATOES)

1 to 2 tablespoons olive oil

2 potatoes, sliced

1 or 2 carrots, sliced

1 handful of fresh or frozen broad beans, shelled

1 small bunch of fresh broad beans in pods (optional)

### FOR THE COOKING STOCK

3 tablespoons tomato paste

½ teaspoon sea salt, or more to taste

½ teaspoon ground black pepper

1 tablespoon vegetable stock powder

2 tablespoons olive oil

2 to 3 tablespoons pomegranate molasses (depending on how sour your molasses is, see Notes)

2 cups (480 mL) boiling water, plus more as needed

CONTINUES

**1. Prepare the veggies for stuffing:** Place the sun-dried peppers in a bowl and cover with boiling water. Let soak for at least 30 minutes, then drain well.

**2.** Cut the zucchini in half and remove the center flesh with a small knife, vegetable corer, or melon baller, trying to remove as much as possible without piercing through the outer layer. Chop the flesh and set aside to add to the filling. Repeat with the eggplant, until you're left with about ¼ to ½ inch (0.6 to 1.25 cm) of the eggplant shell. Chop the flesh and set aside to add to the filling.

**3.** Rinse the grape leaves.

**4.** Cut the ends off the onions, then cut them halfway into the middle from the side (see Notes) and place in a big bowl of hot water for 10 to 15 minutes. Then separate the onion into layers.

**5. Prepare the filling:** Combine all the filling ingredients plus the flesh of the zucchini and eggplant in a large bowl. Taste and adjust the salt, lemon, and spices to your liking (you don't have to chew the uncooked rice; just discard it after tasting).

**6. Prepare the potato layer:** Coat the bottom of a large pot with olive oil and cover with the potatoes, carrots, and broad beans (or all potato) in a single layer.

**7. Stuff the veggies:** The easiest way to roll grape leaves is to lay them flat and place ½ to 1 tablespoon of filling (depending on the size of the leaf) in the center, roll up the bottom part, fold in the edges from the sides, and then roll all the way up. Stuff the other veggies as well, then place them tightly in the pot as you go, with those that require the longest cooking time—in this case, the dried peppers—closer to the bottom and the rest stacked on top. Cover the top with a heatproof plate slightly smaller than the pot; this will create some pressure to prevent the veggies from losing their shape.

**8.** Mix all the ingredients for the stock and pour over the veggies until it just reaches, but doesn't cover, the top layer. If you don't have enough liquid to reach the top layer, top it off with more boiling water.

**9.** Bring to a boil over medium-high heat, cover, and cook for 15 minutes, then reduce the heat to medium-low and simmer until the veggies are tender and the rice is cooked through. Check after 1 hour. If you want more liquid to cook off before serving, uncover the pot and cook for a few more minutes and up to half an hour (although juicy is recommended).

**10.** Traditionally, before serving, cover the pot with a large plate or tray and then flip the pot upside down. If attempting this, please be careful—the pot contains very hot liquid. You can also cover the top of the pot with a large flatbread before covering with the plate and flipping. The bread will soak up the juices.

## NOTES

• *You might not find all the ingredients at your local supermarket, but they can all be found at any Middle Eastern market or ordered online. Otherwise you can substitute with other vegetables of your choosing.*

• *To get the desired amount of cooked lentils, you'll need a little under ½ cup (80 g) dried lentils. Alternatively, you could use 3.5 ounces (100 g) finely chopped walnuts.*

• *If you cannot find pomegranate molasses, you can use cranberry juice concentrate or balsamic vinegar mixed with a little sugar.*

• *When cutting the onion, you're making one large cut without going all the way through, so that you're left with layers of onion that will serve as mini taco-like shells that can then be filled. To see a tutorial of Seiran demonstrating this, go to bestofvegan.com/mycookbook.*

• *The aprax can be served warm or cold. They are really good the day after when the flavors have developed.*

• Aprax *is typically served with* Mast û Xiyar, *Kurdish cucumber salad with garlic, yogurt, and dried mint, easily veganized with vegan Greek-style yogurt.*

"Hey Dilbere" by Ciwan Haco

# SWEDISH PLANT BALLS
## WITH CREAM SAUCE, RAW LINGONBERRY JAM & QUICK-PICKLED CUCUMBERS

**In collaboration with**

Seiran Sinjari, recipe developer and creator of Salt & Tahini (Kurdistan and Sweden)

**Yield: 4 servings**

*Prep time: 20 minutes*
*Cook time: 30 minutes*
*Total time: 50 minutes*

Being of Scandinavian, including Swedish, descent, I reached out to Seiran, who is based in Stockholm, to ask her to share a recipe that would be reminiscent of both my ancestry and the country she's lived in her whole life. The result was these Swedish Plant Balls with the typically creamy sauce that sets them apart from other cultures' meatball dishes (like the Moroccan Veggie Tajine Kefta on page 73).

Seiran remembers eating meatballs at many places, but unlike what most people outside of Sweden believe, the Swedish furniture store Ikea was rarely one of them. The best ones, she said, are served either at home or at fancy and pricey restaurants in downtown Stockholm.

Traditionally, Swedish meatballs are served with a cream sauce, raw lingonberry jam (*rårörda lingon*), and quick-pickled cucumbers (*pressgurka*).

*FOR THE QUICK-PICKLED CUCUMBERS*
1 skinny English cucumber, very thinly sliced (preferably using a mandoline)

½ teaspoon sea salt

2 tablespoons white vinegar

2 tablespoons sugar

1 small pinch of ground white pepper

1 tablespoon finely chopped fresh parsley or dill

*FOR THE LINGONBERRY JAM*
9 ounces (250 g) frozen lingonberries, or fresh if in season (see Notes)

¼ cup (50 g) sugar

*FOR THE PLANT BALLS*
⅓ cup plus 1 tablespoon (95 mL) vegan heavy cream

3 tablespoons fine bread crumbs, plus more if needed for shaping

18 ounces (500 g) vegan mince (suitable for shaping)

1 small yellow onion, grated

1½ to 3 teaspoons spicy brown mustard, coarse mustard, or any other vegan mustard

1 teaspoon ground allspice

¼ teaspoon ground cloves

½ teaspoon ground black pepper

½ teaspoon ground white pepper

1 tablespoon dark soy sauce (preferably Chinese dark mushroom soy sauce)

Sea salt to taste (see Notes)

3 tablespoons vegan butter

*FOR THE CREAM SAUCE*
2 tablespoons vegan butter

2 tablespoons all-purpose flour

⅔ cup (160 mL) vegetable stock, plus more if needed

1 cup (240 mL) vegan heavy cream or coconut cream, plus more if needed

1 tablespoon dark soy sauce (preferably Chinese mushroom soy sauce)

1 tablespoon black currant jelly (optional)

3 whole cloves

Ground black pepper to taste

½ teaspoon balsamic vinegar

*TO SERVE*
Mashed potatoes, potato puree, or boiled potatoes

*CONTINUES*

1.  **Make the quick-pickled cucumbers:** Place the sliced cucumber in a shallow bowl and sprinkle with the salt. Place a plate on top, then set a heavy object on the plate to squeeze out some of the liquid. Let sit for 30 minutes, then drain the cucumbers.

2.  Mix the white vinegar, sugar, and white pepper in a sterilized and airtight glass container until the sugar has dissolved. Add the cucumbers and parsley and stir to combine. Secure the lid and marinate in the refrigerator for at least 30 minutes before serving. The cucumbers can be stored in the fridge for up to 1 week.

3.  **Make the lingonberry jam:** Place the lingonberries in a bowl and combine with the sugar. Let sit at room temperature until the berries have thawed (30 to 60 minutes). Stir every now and then until all the sugar crystals have dissolved. The process is the same for fresh lingonberries; just make sure to break some of the berries when stirring so they release their liquid. (Lingonberries contain benzoic acid, a natural preservative, so if you store the raw jam in a sterilized airtight glass container, it keeps well at room temperature for up to 2 weeks or even longer in the fridge.)

4.  **Make the plant balls:** Place the heavy cream in a small bowl and mix in the bread crumbs. Stir with a fork after 5 minutes and then again after 10 minutes; it should be a thick paste by now.

5.  In a large bowl, combine the vegan mince, onion, mustard, allspice, cloves, black pepper, white pepper, soy sauce, salt, and the heavy cream and bread crumb paste. Mix well using your hands. The mixture should be a little bit sticky, but if it's too wet to form balls, add a little sprinkle of bread crumbs.

6.  Line a baking sheet with parchment paper. Roll the mixture into little balls, using 1 to 1½ tablespoons for each. Wet your hands if the balls are sticking to them. Place the balls on the baking sheet.

7.  Melt about 1 tablespoon of the vegan butter in a large skillet over medium heat and add some of the plant balls (working in 2 or 3 batches so as not to crowd them). Fry until golden brown on all sides and cooked through, about 8 to 10 minutes, shaking the pan frequently. Clean the pan between batches and then add more vegan butter. (Alternatively, you can cook the plant balls in the oven at 400°F/200°C for 15 to 20 minutes. The texture will end up a bit drier than when frying them on the stove.)

8.  **Make the cream sauce:** Melt the vegan butter in a small pan over medium heat, slowly whisk in the flour, and keep whisking for 30 seconds. Slowly add the stock while whisking to avoid lumps. Then slowly add the heavy cream while whisking to create a smooth sauce.

9.  Add the soy sauce, black currant jelly (if using), cloves, and black pepper. Simmer over medium-low heat, stirring frequently, until the sauce has thickened and the jelly has melted. If the sauce is too thick, slowly add some more stock or heavy cream. Add the balsamic vinegar, stir, and remove from the heat. Remove the whole cloves before serving.

10. Serve the Swedish plant balls with mashed potatoes, potato puree, or boiled potatoes together with the cream sauce, quick-pickled cucumbers, and raw lingonberry jam.

## NOTES

• *If you can't find lingonberries, you can use store-bought lingonberry jam (you can find it at any Ikea store).*

• *You may not need any additional salt, as the soy sauce is very savory and vegan mince is typically also seasoned with salt.*

"En säng av rosor"
by Darin

MAIN DISHES

# Wholesome

**I** **LEARNED TO LOVE HEALTHY** foods only after going vegan. Until then, mince and cheese pies, chocolate muffins, frozen pizza, and chicken nuggets were my go-to foods. I'd have spinach on occasion, but only if it was drenched in heavy cream and a lot of salt. I never thought I'd ever learn to like salads, or any kind of fresh produce, really. During my first years as a vegan, I embraced so-called vegan junk food because it allowed me to be vegan without changing everything about my eating habits.

The year before I went vegan, my father died unexpectedly from a heart attack at age fifty-three. The older I get, the more I realize how very young he still was. I was so struck with grief that I couldn't even think about the ways in which my life was headed in the same direction as his. Like him, I numbed my emotions with processed foods and unhealthy lifestyle habits.

When he died, I didn't connect the dots at first. It wasn't until I was into my second year as a vegan that I started looking into plant-based and more wholesome nutrition. I had read somewhere that our taste buds can get used to any taste after just a few weeks, so little by little, I forced myself to eat healthy foods I had previously either never tried or hated, and I learned to love them over time.

In a society so obsessed with clean eating, dieting, and weight loss, I often meet people with the opposite trajectory. They had to teach themselves that it was okay to eat foods that aren't considered healthy because, for instance, they contain sugar or oil. That's why talking about healthy food is often associated with demonizing everything else. That is not my mindset, nor do I believe that it is healthy for us mentally.

I approach health as something holistic that can't be reduced to just what we eat. If obsessing over not eating a donut makes you miserable and prevents you from enjoying your life, then that's not healthy either. Health is the sum of the things we do that make us feel good—physically, mentally, emotionally, and spiritually. Drinking a green smoothie makes me feel good, but so does occasionally having a piece of cake. It's about finding what works best for you. I adore vegetable-centric recipes, adopting low-waste habits, and drinking green juices, but that doesn't mean I don't also enjoy other ways of eating. Furthermore, a healthy lifestyle also means focusing on sleep, reducing our stress levels, moving our bodies, drinking plenty of water, and getting fresh air. Moreover, I love to mix it up and include a little white wine in my asparagus soup, some bread in my salad, or a little extra oil or even whiskey with my sautéed veggies. Hence the term *healthy(ish)* to describe the recipes in this chapter.

**Tip:** For the most accurate information on plant-based nutrition, please refer to registered dietitians. You'll find a list of resources at the end of this book.

# SALTED CHOCOLATE TAHINI SPREAD

Yield: 2 cups (480 mL)
*Prep time: 5 minutes*
*Total time: 5 minutes*

This is my favorite chocolate spread because it's incredibly quick and easy to make and it tastes amazing. I love adding it to a slice of homemade bread and enjoying it with a latte or hot chocolate, usually for breakfast or as an afternoon snack. The flaky salt is optional, but highly recommended!

**1 cup (240 mL) tahini**

**⅔ to 1 cup (160 to 240 mL) maple syrup (see Note)**

**½ cup (50 g) cacao powder**

**1 generous pinch of flaky salt (optional)**

**1.** Using a whisk or fork, mix all the ingredients in a bowl until smooth.

**2.** Transfer to an airtight container and store in the fridge for up to a week.

## NOTE

*For a sweeter and even creamier result, use 1 cup (240 mL) maple syrup.*

"Chocolate" by
Marisa Monte and
"Appletree" by Erykah Badu

# GO-TO GRANOLA

 Yield: 5 servings
*Prep time: 5 minutes*
*Cook time: 15 to 20 minutes*
*Total time: 20 to 25 minutes*

**1¼ cups (115 g) quick oats, gluten-free if desired**

**1¼ cups (187.5 g) mixed unsalted nuts and/or seeds, chopped (see Notes)**

**⅓ cup (60 to 80 g) dried fruit (see Notes)**

**⅓ cup (80 mL) liquid sweetener (see Notes)**

**1 tablespoon seasoning (see Notes)**

**1 pinch of sea salt**

**1 teaspoon vanilla or almond extract (optional)**

**1 tablespoon of sunflower seed oil or melted coconut oil (optional)**

**1.** Preheat the oven to 300°F (150°C) and line a baking tray with parchment paper.

**2.** Mix all the ingredients in a bowl, making sure everything is evenly coated in the sweetener.

**3.** Spread the granola on the baking tray and bake for 15 to 20 minutes, until lightly toasted and crisp.

**4.** Let cool and store in an airtight container in the fridge or pantry for up to 2 months.

## NOTES

• *Nut suggestions: cashews, walnuts, hazelnuts, almonds (whole, chopped, sliced, or slivered), macadamias, pecans, Brazil nuts, peanuts, pine nuts, pistachios.*

• *Seed suggestions: flaxseed, hemp seed, pumpkin seed, sunflower seed, poppy seed, sesame seed, chia seed.*

• *Dried or dehydrated fruit suggestions: raisins, cherries, figs, apricots, mulberries, mangoes, bananas, apples.*

• *Liquid sweetener suggestions: maple syrup, coconut nectar, date syrup, blackstrap molasses.*

• *Seasoning suggestions: cacao powder, pumpkin pie spice, cinnamon.*

• *Feel free to also add vegan chocolate chips once the granola is fully cooled.*

# IRON-RICH HOT CHOCOLATE

**GF**

**LV**

Yield: 1 serving

*Prep time: 5 minutes*
*Cook time: 3 to 4 minutes*
*Total time: 8 to 9 minutes*

**NUTRITION NUGGET:** Blackstrap molasses is rich in minerals such as calcium and iron. Including it consistently in your diet is a good way to work toward meeting your daily iron needs. You can add it to hot drinks like this iron-rich hot chocolate, mix it into your oatmeal or granola, bake with it, or mix it with some lemon juice, apple cider vinegar, and hot water.

1½ cups (360 mL) fortified soy, almond, cashew, or oat milk

1 tablespoon blackstrap molasses (see Note)

1 tablespoon cacao powder

1 tablespoon almond or cashew butter

1 teaspoon maca powder (optional)

1 pinch of sea salt

**1.** Blend all the ingredients in a blender, then transfer to a pot.

**2.** Heat over medium to high heat for 3 to 4 minutes until hot, but not boiling.

## NOTES

• *Blackstrap molasses can take some getting used to, so if you don't like the taste, feel free to either partially or fully substitute with maple syrup or coconut sugar while you adjust to this new flavor.*

• *Maca root has a nutty, butterscotch-like taste, as well as many health benefits, which is why I love adding it to hot drinks and smoothies.*

 "This Feeling" by Alabama Shakes and "River" by Herbie Hancock and Corinne Bailey Rae

# GINGERBREAD LATTE

**GF**

**TNF**

**LV**

In collaboration with

Sarah Kermalli, food photographer and recipe developer, creator of Sculpted Kitchen

Yield: 1½ cups (360 mL)

*Prep time: 5 minutes*
*Total time: 5 minutes*

This drink is perfect for a cozy afternoon at home while reading a book or just relaxing.

1½ cups (360 mL) plant milk (nut-free if desired)

1 to 2 tablespoons maple syrup (depending on your sweet tooth)

¼ teaspoon vanilla powder or extract

½ teaspoon ground cinnamon

½ teaspoon ginger powder (1 teaspoon if you want it spicy!)

1 pinch of ground nutmeg

1 pinch of ground cloves

**1.** Heat the milk to a simmer in a small pot.

**2.** Remove the pot from the heat and stir in the remaining ingredients.

**3.** Garnish with dark chocolate shavings, coconut whipped cream, a cinnamon stick, or a sprinkle of cinnamon.

"Eating nutrient-dense, plant-based foods has given me so much joy and a sense of calm, as well as a new level of compassion that I love to bring to the table and share with others."
—SARAH KERMALLI

FROM LEFT: Protein Green Smoothie, opposite, Vitamin C Booster Smoothie, page 124, Go-To Green Juice, page 124

# PROTEIN GREEN
# SMOOTHIE

Yield: 1 serving
*Prep time: 5 minutes*
*Total time: 5 minutes*

A smoothie is a great and easy way to add more greens and nutrients to your life. Blending everything saves you a lot of time too. I love to carry a thermos around with me and have my smoothies on the go. Here are my top three tips when it comes to smoothies (or, as my grandmother calls them, fruit soups):

1. Make it cold! Add either ice cubes or frozen fruit to your smoothie. It's *so* much better than a room-temperature smoothie, trust me.

2. Make it sweet. You can add sweetness by including fruits like bananas, apples, or mangoes, dried fruits like dates, or even some coconut nectar.

3. Make it flavorful. Some smoothies that are mostly fruit based, like the Vitamin C Booster Smoothie on page 124, don't really need much else because fruits are such flavor bombs. But when it comes to greener or more protein-rich smoothies, I find that adding some cacao powder or peanut butter is a very easy way to instantly make them taste better and overpower any bitterness from the greens.

*BASE*
**1 ripe banana**

**1 scoop vegan protein powder (neutral flavor or vanilla)**

**1 tablespoon peanut butter**

**1 cup (200 g) ice cubes**

**½ to 1½ cups oat or soy milk (depending on your desired consistency)**

**1 cup (30 g) baby spinach**

*OPTIONAL ADD-ONS*
**1 teaspoon spirulina**

**1 teaspoon maca powder**

**1 teaspoon hemp seeds**

Blend all the ingredients, including any desired add-ons, in a high-speed blender until smooth.

**"Time and Place"
by Lee Moses**

Wholesome

BREAKFAST & DRINKS

123

# VITAMIN C BOOSTER
# SMOOTHIE

**Yield: 1 serving**
*Prep time: 5 minutes*
*Total time: 5 minutes*

1 cup (150 g) whole strawberries (with the tops)

1 cup (225 g) frozen pineapple, peach, or mango

1½ cups (360 mL) orange or tangerine juice

3 or 4 fresh basil leaves (optional)

Blend all ingredients in a high-speed blender until smooth.

## LOW-WASTE TIP

*Did you know that you can eat the green tops of strawberries? Many parts of produce that we typically discard are edible, including kiwi skins, pumpkin and potato skins, broccoli stems, and even banana peels and watermelon rinds if you cook them!*

*SEE PHOTO, PAGE 122*

♫ "Golden" by Jill Scott and "Loretta" by Amos Lee

# GO-TO
# GREEN
# JUICE

**Yield: about 4 cups (1 L) of juice, or 2 large servings**
*Prep time: 10 minutes*
*Total time: 10 minutes*

Smoothies or juices? The short answer is both. The longer answer is that smoothies are generally preferable because they contain fiber, which is stripped from juices. Dietary fiber helps to slow the release of glucose into the bloodstream and is associated with digestive and cardiovascular health. Smoothies are a particularly good choice for those who need to be mindful of their blood sugar. On the other hand, juicing makes it possible to consume the micronutrients—such as antioxidants, vitamins, and minerals—from a large amount of produce in a condensed form. Juices are a good option for those who are hoping to maximize micronutrient intake. They're also a helpful option for those who have sensitive digestion, for whom large amounts of dietary fiber can be difficult to process.

2 green apples

1 thumb-size piece of fresh ginger

2 cucumbers

1 bunch of fresh parsley

3 cups (90 g) spinach

3 celery stalks

1 lemon

Wash and chop all the ingredients except the lemon, and juice them using a juicer (for a guide on how to choose the best juicer, go to bestofvegan .com/mycookbook). Remove the lemon peel before adding the lemon to the juicer (no need to peel the other ingredients). If you don't have a juicer, you can also blend the ingredients in a high-speed blender or food processor and then strain the juice through a nut-milk bag or cheesecloth.

*SEE PHOTO, PAGE 122*

# LITTLE CHOC'S BURRITO CREPES

In collaboration with
Julia Kravets, owner of Little Choc
Apothecary

Yield: 4 crepes (4 servings)

*Prep time: 20 minutes*
*Cook time: 15 to 20 minutes*
*Total time: 35 to 40 minutes*

New York City's very first fully vegan creperie was Little Choc Apothecary in Williamsburg, Brooklyn. The first time I ate there in 2015, I was immediately enchanted. The café itself is utterly charming and cute. It's perfect for a coffee or tea date, brunch, a cozy lunch alone or with friends, and even dinner with a good glass of wine. Their crepes come with your choice of either sweet or savory toppings. They also serve smoothies and baked goods. When thinking of vegan restaurants to potentially collaborate with for this book, Little Choc Apothecary was at the top of my list, as it's one of my go-to places whenever I'm back in New York. Having lived in Brooklyn for many years, it was the number one spot I would order lunch from whenever I wasn't in the mood to cook, but still wanted a wholesome, delicious meal. My usual order is the burrito crepe, so I was thrilled when Julia, the owner, agreed to collaborate on this adaptation of her original recipe.

♫ "Hallelujah, I Love Her So" by Ray Charles

## FOR THE CASHEW CHEESE

1½ cups (210 g) raw cashews, soaked for at least 4 to 6 hours, or quick-soaked in boiling water for 10 to 15 minutes, then drained

1 tablespoon olive oil

¾ teaspoon garlic powder

1 teaspoon sea salt

¼ cup (15 g) nutritional yeast

1½ teaspoons apple cider vinegar

1 cup (240 mL) water, plus more if needed

## FOR THE HOT SAUCE

Half of a 7-ounce (200 g) can chipotles in adobo, including adobo

2 garlic cloves

½ cup plus 1 tablespoon (135 mL) water

1 tablespoon apple cider vinegar

1 tablespoon maple syrup

¾ teaspoon ground cumin

½ teaspoon sea salt

## FOR THE CREPES

1½ cups (187.5 g) all-purpose flour (or gluten-free all-purpose flour plus ½ teaspoon xanthan gum)

2 cups (480 mL) sparkling water

1 tablespoon vegan butter, melted, plus more for cooking

1 pinch of sea salt

## TOPPINGS

¾ cup (50 g) Coconut Bacon (page 209)

2 ripe avocados, peeled, pitted, and sliced

2 cups (350 g) cooked black beans, reheated

**1. Make the cashew cheese:** Blend all the ingredients in a high-speed bender until smooth. If the cheese is too thick, add a bit more water to reach the desired consistency.

**2. Make the hot sauce:** Blend all the ingredients thoroughly, then pour the sauce into a small saucepan and simmer over medium-low heat until reduced and thickened a little, about 5 to 10 minutes.

**3. Make the crepes:** Whisk all the ingredients until you get a smooth batter. Heat a little vegan butter in a large nonstick skillet over medium heat. When the skillet is hot, add about ½ to ¾ cup (120 to 180 mL) of the batter into the pan using a small ladle. Move the pan around immediately to spread the batter across the whole surface and ensure the crepe isn't too thick.

**4.** Cook for 2 to 3 minutes on each side (flip when little bubbles start forming). The crepe should start turning golden brown. Repeat with the remaining batter. Transfer each crepe to a plate.

**5.** Add the toppings to the crepes, fold, and serve. Any leftover hot sauce can be kept in the fridge for later use.

GFO

HP

Wholesome

BREAKFAST & DRINKS

# TOFU & VEGGIE BREAKFAST WRAP

**Yield: 4 servings/wraps**

*Prep time: 10 minutes*
*Cook time: 25 minutes*
*Total time: 35 minutes*

If you don't love tofu, you probably just haven't found the right way to prepare it yet! Grating or scrambling tofu and then cooking it with veggies and spices can be both flavorful and very filling given tofu's high protein content. Feel free to customize this recipe to your liking.

Wholesome

BREAKFAST & DRINKS

1 tablespoon olive oil

8 ounces (225 g) extra-firm tofu, pressed (see Notes)

1 small onion, diced

1 small sweet potato, peeled and diced, about 1½ cups (187.5 g)

1 cup (100 g) mushrooms of choice, thinly sliced

1 green or red bell pepper, chopped

2 scallions, chopped

2 garlic cloves, minced

1 teaspoon turmeric powder

1 teaspoon paprika

1 teaspoon ground cumin

1 teaspoon dried thyme

¼ teaspoon chili powder (optional)

1 pinch cayenne pepper or red pepper flakes (optional)

½ to ¾ teaspoon sea salt or celery salt, or to taste

½ to 1 teaspoon kala namak (black salt), or to taste

2 cups (60 g) baby spinach, packed, or chopped kale

Juice of 1 lime (about 2 tablespoons), or to taste

2 tablespoons nutritional yeast (optional)

½ cup (120 mL) water

*TO SERVE*

4 medium tortilla wraps, gluten-free if desired

1 avocado, peeled, pitted, and cubed

½ cup (115 g) cherry tomatoes, halved

½ handful of fresh cilantro

Your favorite vegan dip or sauce

**1.** In a large nonstick pan, warm the olive oil over medium heat. Add the onion, sweet potato, mushrooms, bell pepper, scallions, and garlic and sauté for 10 minutes. Stir in the spices at the 5-minute mark (see Notes).

**2.** In the meantime, grate the tofu using a cheese grater, or crumble it in a bowl using a fork or your hands.

**3.** Add the tofu to the pan and cook for 10 minutes, or until the diced sweet potato is tender, gradually adding the water while cooking mixing in the spinach, lime juice, and nutritional yeast toward the end.

**4.** Heat the wraps in a small skillet if desired. Fill them with the tofu mix, avocado, tomatoes, and cilantro.

**5.** Fold up and enjoy with your favorite vegan dip or sauce.

## NOTES

• *To press the tofu, either use a tofu press or place the block of tofu between two plates, adding a heavy object like a book or dumbbell on top for a few minutes. You can use black beans or kidney beans instead of tofu.*

• *If you're short on time, you can use all-purpose seasoning instead of the spices listed here.*

 "Spanish Joint" by D'Angelo

# CREAM OF ASPARAGUS SOUP

Yield: 2 servings

Prep time: 10 minutes
Cook time: 25 minutes
Total time: 35 minutes

This recipe is inspired by the soup my mother used to make at least once a week when I was little. She'd usually add a lot of heavy cream and some sausage; this is a lighter vegan version. I also added some white wine for a little extra pep.

"Tout Va Bien" by Lokua Kanza and "The Wind" by Yusuf/Cat Stevens

**FOR THE SOUP**

**18 ounces (500 g) white asparagus (green asparagus works too)**

**2 yellow or white onions, chopped**

**4 garlic cloves, minced**

**2 tablespoons vegan butter or olive oil**

**¼ cup (60 mL) white wine or water**

**2 teaspoons vegetable bouillon base or powder, such as Better Than Bouillon (see Note)**

**1 14-ounce (400 mL) can full-fat coconut milk**

**Juice of ½ lemon (1 tablespoon)**

**Sea salt and ground black pepper to taste**

**TO SERVE**

**Drizzle of olive oil**

**Freshly cracked pepper**

**Sea salt (optional)**

**Chopped fresh chives, basil leaves, and/or dill (optional)**

**Shiitake bacon (recipe on page 209) (optional)**

**Toasted sourdough bread, gluten-free if desired, with vegan butter**

**1.** Peel the asparagus using a vegetable peeler (no need to peel green asparagus) and cut off and discard the bottom ½ inch (1.25 cm) of the stems (not the tips!). Chop the asparagus and put it in a medium saucepan with the onions, garlic, and vegan butter.

**2.** Sauté over medium to high heat for 9 minutes, stirring frequently to make sure nothing burns. At the 9-minute mark, add the white wine and cook for another minute.

**3.** Add the vegetable bouillon base and coconut milk. Stir the soup, cover, reduce the heat to medium-low, and simmer for 15 minutes.

**4.** Remove the pot from the heat, mix in the lemon juice, and blend the soup using an immersion blender.

**5.** Taste for seasoning and add salt and/or pepper if needed.

**6.** Pour the soup into 2 bowls. Drizzle with olive oil and garnish with a little cracked pepper, sea salt (if using), shiitake bacon, and/or fresh herbs. Serve with toasted and buttered bread.

## NOTE

*The exact amount of bouillon base will depend on the brand you are using; just follow the label directions for 2 cups (480 mL) of liquid.*

GFO

TNF

 LV

Wholesome

SOUPS & SALADS

# ROASTED GARLIC & BUTTER BEAN SOUP
## WITH BASIL & THYME

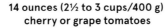

### Yield: 2 servings

*Prep time: 5 minutes*
*Cook time: 30 minutes*
*Total time: 35 minutes*

GF
TNF
LV
HP

Wholesome

SOUPS & SALADS

Adding beans to your soup is one of the best ways to make it more filling and also include more protein and fiber. My main goal here was to create a soup recipe that didn't include broth or cream, so you can taste the full depth of flavor from the vegetables. I love the combination of bell pepper and tomato, but if you'd like a more traditional tomato soup taste, you can simply omit the bell peppers and add more tomatoes instead. This soup is great served with toasted sourdough bread with vegan butter or with Jalapeño Popper Grilled Cheese (page 39). Recipe note: Only half of the soup ingredients are blended. Be sure to read all instructions carefully.

- 14 ounces (2½ to 3 cups/400 g) cherry or grape tomatoes
- 1 medium to large shallot, roughly chopped (or ½ small yellow or red onion)
- 1 medium red bell pepper, stem and seeds removed, cut into wedges
- 1 or 2 whole garlic heads (depending on how much garlic you prefer), outermost papery layer removed and top ¼ inch sliced off, exposing the cloves
- ½ to 1 teaspoon grated fresh ginger, peeled, or ¼ teaspoon ginger powder
- 2 tablespoons olive oil
- ½ teaspoon sea salt
- 1 teaspoon coconut sugar
- ¼ teaspoon smoked paprika
- ⅛ teaspoon cayenne pepper (use less or just omit if you like it less spicy)
- 2 cracks of black pepper
- 1 14-ounce (400 g) can butter beans or other white beans (but *not* green, mature lima beans), rinsed and drained
- 1 small handful of fresh thyme sprigs
- Juice of ½ lemon (1 tablespoon)
- 1 handful of fresh basil leaves

### TO SERVE
Toasted sourdough bread (or gluten-free bread) with vegan butter (optional)

**1.** Preheat the oven to 350°F (180°C).

**2.** Arrange the ingredients on a large baking tray at least 1 inch (2.5 cm) deep as follows: On one side, place half the cherry tomatoes, the shallot, bell pepper, garlic, ginger, 1 tablespoon olive oil, ¼ teaspoon sea salt, coconut sugar, smoked paprika, cayenne pepper, and 2 cracks of black pepper. On the other side, arrange the butter beans, the rest of the cherry tomatoes, olive oil, sea salt, and the fresh thyme. Stir both sides separately to make sure everything is well coated in oil and seasonings.

**3.** Roast for 30 minutes, until the vegetables are tender.

**4.** Using a ladle or serving spoon, transfer the bell pepper and garlic side of the tray into a blender. Squeeze the roasted garlic cloves from the bulbs directly into the blender, discarding the remaining layer of the bulb (use a kitchen towel to prevent burning yourself). Add the lemon juice and blend until smooth, then transfer to 2 bowls.

**5.** Top with the rest of the ingredients from the other side of the baking tray (the seasoned butter beans and the other half of the tomatoes, including all liquids, but removing the bigger thyme twigs) and the fresh basil leaves.

**6.** Serve the soup as is or with a slice of toasted sourdough bread with vegan butter.

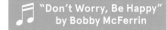

"Don't Worry, Be Happy" by Bobby McFerrin

132

# WHITE BEAN SALAD
## WITH MISO-GINGER DRESSING

Yield: 1 large or 2 small servings

*Prep time: 15 minutes*
*Cook time: 5 minutes*
*Total time: 20 minutes*

Beans (and other legumes) are a true superfood and should be a staple in every vegan kitchen. They're inexpensive, easy to prepare, tasty, filling, high in protein and fiber, and, depending on the kind of bean, rich in iron, folate, manganese, and copper. This salad combines tasty white beans with the fruitiness of strawberries, the nutiness of pine nuts, and a deliciously refreshing miso-ginger dressing.

 **"The Obvious Child"**
**by Paul Simon**

*FOR THE BEANS*
**2 teaspoons olive oil**

**¼ cup (35 g) pine nuts**

**2 scallions, white parts only, chopped, green parts reserved for the salad**

**1 14-ounce (400 g) can white beans (or butter beans or cannellini beans), drained and rinsed (see Notes)**

**½ teaspoon garlic powder or 1 garlic clove, minced**

**¼ teaspoon sea salt, or to taste**

**1 pinch of freshly cracked pepper**

*FOR THE DRESSING*
**1 tablespoon light miso paste or chickpea miso**

**Juice of ½ lemon (1 tablespoon)**

**1 tablespoon water**

**1 tablespoon maple syrup**

**1 tablespoon olive oil**

**1 teaspoon apple cider vinegar**

**½ teaspoon minced or grated fresh ginger, or more to taste**

*FOR THE SALAD*
**3 to 4 cups (90 to 120 g) fresh baby spinach**

**1 ripe avocado, peeled, pitted, and cubed**

**2 radishes, thinly sliced (optional)**

**1 cup fresh strawberries (150 g), sliced or quartered (no need to remove the green part!) (see Notes)**

**Juice of ½ lemon (about 1 tablespoon)**

**Chopped fresh parsley and chives, for garnish (optional)**

**1.** For the beans, heat the olive oil in a nonstick pan and add the pine nuts once the pan is hot. Toast the pine nuts over medium-high heat for 2 minutes, then add the white parts of the scallions, beans, garlic, salt, and pepper. Cook for 2 to 3 more minutes, until warmed through. Set aside to cool down a little.

**2.** While the beans cool, make the dressing by blending all the ingredients using an immersion blender or small food processor. (You can mix it using a fork or whisk too, but the result will be a little less creamy.)

**3.** Mix the beans with the salad ingredients and serve with the miso-ginger dressing. Best enjoyed immediately.

## NOTES
• *Chickpeas, tempeh, or tofu would work in this recipe too. If you're allergic to legumes, you can use cooked quinoa instead.*

• *If strawberries are out of season or not available, you can use raisins, dried cranberries, or dried cherries instead.*

## LOW-WASTE TIP
*If you don't want to buy beans in cans or jars, you can purchase them dried in bulk (some stores allow you to bring your own containers), then cook them in a pressure cooker and either store them in the fridge for a few days or in the freezer for a few months. (If you freeze your beans, be sure to first freeze them on a lined baking tray and then transfer them to another container. They're much easier to separate and measure once frozen.) You can find a legume cooking guide with exact cooking times by type of bean at bestofvegan.com/mycookbook.*

GF

LV

HP

Wholesome

SOUPS & SALADS

# WARM BALSAMIC BELUGA LENTIL SALAD

Yield: 2 to 4 servings (see Notes)

Prep time: 10 minutes
Cook time: 20 minutes
Total time: 30 minutes

Beluga lentils are a variety of small black lentils named after beluga caviar, which they resemble only visually. They don't get as soft as other lentils, so they're wonderful in salads, but not ideal in soups. I recommend using beluga lentils for this recipe, but if you can't find them, dark green French lentils are the next best option.

🎵 "Summer Girl" by Haim

SOUPS & SALADS
Wholesome
GF
LV
HP

**FOR THE LENTILS**

⅔ cup (145 g) beluga lentils

2½ cups (600 mL) water

¼ teaspoon sea salt, plus more to taste

**FOR THE DRESSING**

Juice of 1 lemon (about 2 tablespoons)

3 tablespoons balsamic reduction, plus more as needed (see Notes)

1 tablespoon olive oil

1 teaspoon garlic powder

½ teaspoon onion powder

Sea salt to taste

Ground black pepper to taste

**FOR THE SALAD**

1.5 ounces (43 g) whole unsalted almonds, toasted (see Notes)

5.5 ounces (155 g) grape tomatoes, cut in half

1½ cups (30 g) arugula (or more if making 4 servings; see Notes)

2 cups (60 g) baby spinach (or more if making 4 servings; see Notes)

½ small red onion, thinly sliced, optional

1 ripe avocado, peeled, pitted, and cubed

**1. Prepare the lentils:** Rinse the lentils and put them in a pot with the water. Bring to a boil, then cover and simmer over medium heat for about 20 minutes, until the lentils are al dente and the water is completely absorbed, adding more water as necessary.

**2.** Once the lentils are cooked, add in the salt and transfer to a large bowl.

**3. Make the dressing:** In a small bowl, combine the balsamic reduction, lemon juice, olive oil, and spices. Mix the dressing into the lentils with all the salad ingredients, adding the avocado at the very end. Taste and add an extra pinch of salt and/or balsamic reduction if needed.

## NOTES

• *This recipe makes two very filling servings. If you want to make more servings and also turn it into a lighter salad, simply make the same recipe but double or even triple the amount of greens.*

• *If you choose to toast the almonds yourself, simply heat 1 teaspoon olive oil in a small nonstick skillet and add the almonds once the pan is hot. Toast them over medium-high heat for about 2 minutes. Watch and stir them constantly so they don't burn.*

• *Balsamic reduction is recommended because it's thicker, but balsamic vinegar works too. Start with 2 tablespoons, then add more to taste.*

# CHICKPEA CAESAR SALAD

Yield: 2 large or 4 small servings

*Prep time: 10 minutes*
*Cook time: 15 minutes*
*Total time: 25 minutes*

I think we can all agree that lettuce by itself can be quite boring. The trick is to combine it with a creamy and/or tangy dressing and to add some delicious toppings or even bread to the mix. This recipe is simple and a great option for anyone who doesn't usually like salads.

**FOR THE SALAD**

2 14-ounce (400 g) cans chickpeas, drained and rinsed

3 tablespoons olive oil

5.25 ounces (150 g) ciabatta, sourdough, or baguette, cut into chunks

3 tablespoons panko bread crumbs (optional)

2 teaspoons garlic powder

½ teaspoon sea salt

1 pinch of ground black pepper

1 large head of romaine lettuce, roughly chopped (about 4 cups/400 g)

1 pinch of ground black pepper

¼ cup (30 g) capers

**FOR THE DRESSING**

Juice of 1 lemon (2 tablespoons)

½ cup (120 mL) vegan mayo

2 teaspoons olive oil

1 teaspoon Dijon mustard

1 teaspoon red wine vinegar

2 tablespoons nutritional yeast

1½ teaspoons maple syrup

2 garlic cloves, minced, or 1 teaspoon garlic powder

**1.** Preheat the oven to 400°F (200°C) and line a baking tray with parchment paper.

**2.** In a large bowl, mix the chickpeas with the olive oil, bread, bread crumbs (if using), garlic powder, salt, and pepper. Mix well, then transfer to the baking tray and bake for 15 minutes, or until the bread is golden and crispy.

**3.** Mix the dressing ingredients and serve with the lettuce, capers, and chickpea mix.

## NOTE
*This salad can be eaten warm, but if you'd prefer for your lettuce not to get too warm, simply let the chickpea mix cool a bit before serving.*

Wholesome

"Rock Steady" by Aretha Franklin

SOUPS & SALADS

# AVOCADO PESTO PASTA

Yield: 2 servings

*Prep time: 5 minutes*
*Cook time: 10 minutes*
*Total time: 15 minutes*

This quick and easy recipe is a personal favorite and was much loved by the recipe testers as well. It's perfect for a satisfying weeknight dinner or a comforting lunch.

7 ounces (200 g) of your favorite dry pasta (gluten-free if desired)

*FOR THE AVOCADO PESTO SAUCE*

¼ cup (35 g) pine nuts or walnuts

1 packed cup (20 to 30 g) fresh basil leaves

1 packed cup (about 30 g) fresh baby spinach leaves

¼ cup (60 mL) olive oil

¼ cup (60 mL) water

1 ripe avocado, pit and peel removed

Juice of 1 lemon (about 2 tablespoons)

¼ cup (15 g) nutritional yeast

2 garlic cloves

1 teaspoon sea salt, or to taste

1 pinch of ground black pepper

*FOR THE TOPPINGS*

¼ cup (35 g) pine nuts

Fresh basil leaves

Grated vegan parmesan cheese (optional)

**1.** Cook the pasta according to the package instructions.

**2.** Meanwhile, in a small food processor, process the pine nuts, basil, and spinach using the pulse function until finely chopped but not pureed, then add all the other sauce ingredients and process until the sauce is blended yet still slightly chunky. Set aside.

**3.** While the pasta is still cooking, heat a small nonstick pan over high heat. Once the pan is hot, add the pine nuts for the topping and toast until they're just golden brown (but not too dark). This should take only 1 to 2 minutes, so watch carefully and move them around the pan so they get toasted evenly.

**4.** Drain the pasta, transfer to a bowl, mix in the sauce, and top with the toasted pine nuts, fresh basil, and vegan parmesan cheese, if using.

## LOW-WASTE TIP

*This recipe uses a whole avocado, but if you ever need only half an avocado for a recipe, leave the pit in the half you're not using. Then fill a small bowl with water (just enough for the pit and the green part of the avocado to be submerged), place the avocado half in the bowl (cut side down), and store in the fridge. This will keep the avocado from turning brown too quickly.*

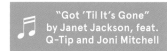

"Got 'Til It's Gone" by Janet Jackson, feat. Q-Tip and Joni Mitchell

# CREAMY VEGGIE PASTA

*Prep time: 10 minutes*
*Cook time: 20 minutes*
*Total time: 30 minutes*

This is a recipe I make every autumn. Yellow and orange leaves, pumpkin spice–scented candles, sweater weather—I love everything about this season. But nothing beats a cozy homecooked late lunch or early dinner. This creamy veggie pasta is soothing and comforting with a creamy cashew miso sauce and crispy veggies. The nutritional yeast gives it a nutty cheese flavor and adds extra protein and B vitamins. If you'd like to add even more protein, use lentil or chickpea pasta.

## FOR THE SAUCE

1 tablespoon olive oil

1 cup (about 150 g) diced butternut squash, with the skin

1½ cups (210 g) unsalted raw cashews

1 red bell pepper, seeded and chopped

1 small yellow or white onion, chopped

2 garlic cloves, chopped

½ teaspoon paprika or smoked paprika

1 pinch each of sea salt and ground black pepper, or more to taste

¾ cup (180 mL) water

1 tablespoon white miso paste or chickpea miso (optional)

1½ cups (360 mL) unsweetened plant milk of choice (such as oat or cashew)

Juice of ½ lemon (1 tablespoon)

¼ cup (15 g) nutritional yeast

## FOR THE PASTA AND VEGGIES

5 ounces (150 g) dry pasta of choice

1 tablespoon olive oil (use less if your sun-dried tomatoes are oil-packed)

4 cups (500 to 700 g) of your favorite mixed veggies (such as broccoli, cauliflower, bell pepper, carrot, zucchini), sliced or chopped into bite-size pieces

2 garlic cloves, sliced

3.5 ounces (100 g) sun-dried tomatoes

1 pinch of sea salt (omit if your sun-dried tomatoes are salted)

Fresh herbs (like chives, basil, or parsley), chopped, for garnish (optional)

Red pepper flakes, for garnish (optional)

**GFO**

Wholesome

PASTA & OTHER MAIN DISHES

*CONTINUES*

143

1. **Make the sauce:** Heat the olive oil in a large pot over medium heat, then add the squash, cashews, bell pepper, onion, garlic, paprika, and salt and pepper. Sauté for 2 to 3 minutes, then add ¼ cup (60 mL) of the water, and cook for another 5 minutes.

2. Stir well to make sure the mixture doesn't burn. Add the remaining ½ cup (120 mL) water and cook for 5 more minutes over high heat, then set aside.

3. Transfer the sauce ingredients to a blender along with the miso paste (if using), milk, lemon juice, and nutritional yeast. Blend on the highest speed until smooth. Taste, add a little more salt if needed, and set aside.

4. **Meanwhile, prepare the pasta and veggies:** Bring a large pot of lightly salted water to a boil and cook the pasta according to the package instructions until al dente (this should take 6 to 9 minutes, depending on the kind of pasta you're using). Drain and set aside.

5. Start sautéing the vegetables while the pasta cooks. Heat the olive oil in a large nonstick skillet over medium-high heat. Add the veggies, garlic, sun-dried tomatoes, and salt and sauté until crispy, 8 to 10 minutes.

6. Once everything is ready, serve the pasta in bowls with the veggies and sauce (see Notes). Garnish with some fresh herbs and red pepper flakes, if desired.

**NOTES**

• *I highly recommend that you not mix the sauce and pasta in the pot, but wait until serving time. The starch from the pasta will thicken the sauce too much.*

• *You can store any leftovers in the fridge for a few days or in the freezer for a few months. Make sure you mix in a little more water or plant milk when you reheat them.*

"Apple Scruffs" by George Harrison

# SWEET POTATO GNOCCHI
## WITH WHIPPED PESTO & MUSHROOMS

In collaboration with

Adam Kenworthy,
plant-based chef, winner of
Food Network's
*Chopped* in 2017

Yield: 2 servings

*Prep time: 30 minutes*
*Cook time: 1 hour, 10 minutes*
*Total time: 1 hour, 40 minutes*

I met Adam Kenworthy in early 2015, the year after I moved to New York. We became friends and then also ended up being neighbors in downtown Manhattan for a few years. I always enjoy cooking with Adam, who's a chef and videographer, and love and admire his creativity. He likes to inspire people who don't usually cook to go out there and experiment with new ingredients.

"I think the best way to start is to just go to the farmers market or a local store where you feel like you can get good produce," Adam says. "Go find something that makes you think, 'Wow, this looks interesting or different.' Watermelon radishes or different types of beets are a great example. You can find any produce you've never even heard of and then just look for recipes online. The whole process of making food for yourself and eating healthy has to be fun. I really just want to encourage everyone to experiment and make it fun. Don't look at it as a task, because then it's going to be a drag and you'll prefer eating out, but if you look at it as a 'Fun Friday Night Dinner' with a movie, you can incorporate some friends into the mix, some music, some stories. It's all about making the experience and eating fun."

*FOR THE GNOCCHI*

2 medium sweet potatoes (16 to 18 ounces/450 to 500 g)

1½ cups (187.5 g) all-purpose flour, more to dust (see Note for a gluten-free option)

1 tablespoon tapioca flour or cornstarch

½ teaspoon sea salt

*FOR THE PESTO*

3 tablespoons walnuts, chopped

1 cup (25 g) fresh basil leaves, packed

⅓ cup (80 mL) extra-virgin olive oil

Juice of ½ lemon (1 tablespoon)

2 tablespoons nutritional yeast

1 garlic clove

⅛ teaspoon sea salt, or to taste

1 pinch of ground black pepper

*FOR THE MUSHROOMS*

8 ounces (225 g) king oyster or maitake mushrooms

2 tablespoons vegan butter or olive oil

4 to 6 fresh thyme sprigs

1 pinch of sea salt

Ground black pepper, to taste

4 garlic cloves, thinly sliced

**GfO**

Wholesome

PASTA & OTHER MAIN DISHES

*CONTINUES*

1. **Make the gnocchi:** Preheat the oven to 425°F (220ºC) and line a baking tray with parchment paper.

2. Place the sweet potatoes on the tray and bake for 45 to 50 minutes, until tender when pierced with a knife.

3. Once ready, let the sweet potatoes cool entirely (place them in the fridge to cool faster).

4. **Meanwhile, make the pesto:** Put all the pesto ingredients in a small blender or mini food processor and mix until smooth, then set aside.

5. Bring a large pot of lightly salted water to a boil. Once the sweet potatoes have cooled down, scoop the flesh into a ricer, discard the skins, and puree the flesh into a bowl. If you don't have a ricer, you can mash them using a potato masher or a fork. Add half of the flour, the tapioca flour, and the salt and mix. Gradually add the remaining flour, but do not overmix or the dough will become sticky and require more flour. The goal is to use as little flour as possible so that the gnocchi don't become too chewy.

6. Briefly knead the dough into a smooth ball, then cut it into four equal parts. Roll each part on a floured surface using your hands until you're left with a strand that's about ½ inch (1.25 cm) in diameter. Cut the strand into about 1-inch (2.5 cm) long gnocchi and immediately add them to the pot of boiling water. Cook for 3 to 4 minutes, or until they easily rise to the top. You may need to do this in 2 batches depending on the size of your pot. Scoop the gnocchi out with a slotted spoon and drain on paper towels.

7. For the mushrooms: If using king oyster mushrooms, slice them lengthwise, then score them on one side with a diamond pattern in order for them to absorb the flavors more easily. If using maitake mushrooms, leave them whole if they are small, or slice them if they are bigger.

8. Melt the vegan butter in a large skillet over medium to high heat, add the mushrooms, thyme sprigs, salt, and pepper, and sauté for 5 minutes. Flip them, then add the garlic and gnocchi and sauté for 5 to 7 minutes more, until both the mushrooms and the gnocchi are crispy. Remove the thyme sprigs before serving the gnocchi and mushrooms with the pesto.

**NOTE**

*For a gluten-free gnocchi option, replace the all-purpose flour and tapioca flour with ¾ cup (97 g) cassava flour (not to be confused with tapioca flour), plus more if needed. Note that you will need significantly less flour for this option and you don't have to be as careful not to overmix or overknead. Add a little more cassava flour if necessary, but be careful not to add too much. Follow all other steps as indicated.*

"Funkier Than a Mosquito's Tweeter" by Nina Simone

# QUICK & EASY ONE-POT
# LEMON
# TAHINI PENNE

**Yield: 1 serving**

*Prep time: 5 minutes*
*Cook time: 10 minutes*
*Total time: 15 minutes*

Tahini is a paste you get from grinding sesame seeds. It's originally a Persian staple that has been gaining in popularity in many other parts of the world as well. You can mix it into a salad dressing or use it to make pasta sauces creamier, making it a great substitute for cashews.

3 ounces (85 g) lentil or chickpea pasta (or any pasta of your choice if not gluten-free)

1 cup (240 mL) vegetable broth

2½ packed cups (75 g) baby spinach

2 tablespoons tahini, or more for an even creamier sauce

Juice of 1 lemon (2 tablespoons)

2 tablespoons plus 1½ teaspoons nutritional yeast

1 teaspoon garlic powder

½ teaspoon onion powder

1 teaspoon white miso paste or umami vegetable seasoning sauce (see Note)

Sea salt and ground black pepper to taste

1 pinch of red pepper flakes, for garnish (optional)

**1.** Cook the pasta according to the package instructions until al dente. Drain.

**2.** Reduce the heat to medium-low and return the drained pasta to the pot.

**3.** Stir in the vegetable broth, spinach, tahini, lemon juice, nutritional yeast, garlic powder, onion powder, and miso paste. Mix well and cook for 1 or 2 minutes, until everything is well incorporated and the miso paste is fully dissolved. Season with salt and pepper.

**4.** Garnish with red pepper flakes, if desired, and serve.

## NOTE
*You can use vegetable bouillon base, such as Better Than Bouillon or Yondu umami seasoning sauce, or just an extra pinch of sea salt.*

 "Junie" by Solange

GF

INF

LV

HP

Wholesome

PASTA & OTHER MAIN DISHES

149

# THE OLD-SCHOOL BOWL

## In collaboration with

Gena Hamshaw, registered dietitian, cookbook author, and founder of the Full Helping

Yield: 1 large or 2 small servings

*Prep time: 10 minutes*
*Cook time: 25 minutes*
*Total time: 35 minutes*

Gena and I have both been vegan for over ten years. One of the things we bonded over from the moment we met in New York many years ago is our love for a good, old-school vegetable bowl, sometimes referred to as a "macro bowl." This simple yet flavorful and nutritious recipe is an homage to the veggie bowls that came long before veganism was ever trendy or fancy.

♪ "Back in the Day" by Erykah Badu

½ cup (75 g) sliced carrots

1 cup (115 g) sliced pumpkin or squash, with the skin, seeds removed

2 cups (75 g) chopped collard greens (or bok choy)

½ cup (85 g) cooked black beans

1 pinch each of salt and ground black pepper, plus more to taste

1 pinch of garlic powder

2 to 4 ounces (60 to 120 g) tempeh, depending on how much you'd like (optional)

1 teaspoon olive oil (optional)

½ cup (100 g) cooked brown rice

### FOR THE DRESSING

4½ teaspoons tahini

Juice of 1 lime (about 2 tablespoons)

1½ teaspoons apple cider vinegar

2 tablespoons water

4½ teaspoons nutritional yeast

4½ teaspoons finely chopped fresh cilantro

1 pinch of sea salt

¾ teaspoon garlic powder

**1.** Steam the carrots in a steamer pot for 10 minutes, then add the pumpkin and steam them together for another 10 minutes. If you don't have a steamer pot, you can also roast them in the oven at 400°F (200°C) for 35 minutes and sauté the greens in a nonstick pan over medium heat with either a little oil or water for 3 to 5 minutes, until just tender. Add the collard greens to the steamer pot and steam everything for 5 more minutes.

**2.** If using canned black beans, rinse and drain them. Place the beans in a small pot along with a pinch each of salt, pepper, and garlic powder and warm over medium heat for 2 to 3 minutes.

**3.** If you're adding tempeh, slice it and sauté in a nonstick pan with the olive oil over medium heat, adding salt and pepper to taste, for 3 to 4 minutes on each side, or until light golden.

**4.** Place the carrots, pumpkin, collards, beans, tempeh (if using), and brown rice in separate piles in a large bowl. To make the dressing, whisk all the ingredients in a small bowl and serve alongside your old-school veggie bowl.

# BROCCOLI STEM
# FRIED RICE

In collaboration with

Max La Manna, low-
waste chef and
cookbook author

Yield: 2 servings

Prep time: 15 minutes
Cook time: 65 minutes
Total time: 1 hour,
20 minutes

Wholesome

PASTA & OTHER MAIN DISHES

Max and I met in New York a few years ago at an event hosted by Gaz Oakley (whose recipe for Welsh Rarebits you can find on page 56) and soon realized that we had a few good friends in common, including Rens Kroes, who is a part of this book as well. Max's passion for reducing food waste and educating people on the environmental impact of our food choices, and his large Instagram following, inspire me endlessly. Following the theme of his first book, *More Plants Less Waste*, here are five of Max's top tips to help you easily reduce food waste.

*1. Shop smart by creating a list:* Then buy only what you need from your list. Even better—first take stock of the food you already have at home.

*2. Save leftovers:* Leftovers aren't just for the holidays. If you happen to cook a lot and you regularly have leftovers, designate a day to use up any that have accumulated in the fridge. It's a great way to avoid throwing away food.

*3. Make friends with your freezer:* Freezing food is one of the easiest ways to preserve it, and the types of food that take well to freezing are endless. You can freeze leftovers from meals, excess produce from your favorite farm stand, bread or bread crumbs, and bulk meals like soups and chilis. It's a great way to ensure you always have a healthy, home-cooked meal available.

*4. Pack your lunch:* A helpful way to save money while reducing your carbon footprint is to bring your lunch to work with you. If you're strapped for time in the morning, try freezing your leftovers in portion-sized containers. That way, you'll have premade, hearty lunches ready to go each morning.

*5. Make homemade stock:* Each week, I keep a container next to my chopping board and toss in any leftover bits or scraps. Eventually, that container is full of amazing scraps that can be used to make a delicious stock. In a saucepan combine the likes of garlic and onion peelings, hearty kale stems, the bottom woody part of asparagus, and any other leftover veg bits. Next, add water, peppercorns, salt, dried seasonings such as thyme or rosemary, and bring to a boil, then reduce heat to low and let everything simmer into an aromatic vegetable broth for about 40 minutes. Store in a sealed jar or container.

1 cup (150 g) wild rice (see Note)

2½ to 3 cups (600 to 720 mL) water, or as needed for your rice

½ teaspoon sea salt

2 tablespoons olive oil

4 garlic cloves, thinly sliced

1 thumb-size piece of fresh ginger, grated

8.5 ounces (240 g) shiitake or oyster mushrooms, sliced

1 large broccoli stem, shredded and/or thinly sliced

1 carrot, shredded

¼ purple cabbage, shredded or chopped (optional)

1 to 2 tablespoons (to taste) gluten-free tamari (or soy sauce if you're not gluten-free)

Sea salt and ground black pepper, to taste

*TO SERVE*
Chopped fresh cilantro

Chopped fresh chives

1 pinch of red pepper flakes

Lemon juice (about 1 to 2 tablespoons or to taste)

1. Rinse the rice and add to a pot with the water and salt. Bring to a boil, then cover with a lid, reduce the heat to low, and let simmer for 35 to 45 minutes, until the rice is chewy and the water has evaporated. The amount of water needed and exact cooking time will vary based on the kind of rice you're using, so be sure to read and follow the package's instructions for the best result.

2. While the rice is cooking, heat the oil in a large pan over medium heat, then add the garlic and ginger and sauté for 2 minutes before adding the mushrooms. Stir and cook for 5 to 7 minutes, until the mushrooms are soft. Next, add the broccoli stem, carrot, and cabbage and cook for 3 to 5 minutes.

3. Add the cooked rice, tamari, and salt and pepper to taste, and cook for 5 minutes, stirring occasionally. If the rice sticks to the pan, add a splash of water or oil.

4. Transfer the fried rice to a plate, garnish with cilantro and chives, and season with red pepper flakes and lemon juice.

### NOTE

*You may use quick-cooking white or brown rice instead. Or, even better, use leftover rice.*

 "Satisfied Mind" by Ben Harper and The Blind Boys of Alabama

# ROASTED
# MAPLE
# PECAN
# BUTTERNUT
# SQUASH

In collaboration with

Ashton Ragsdale, food activist and
recipe builder

Yield: 2 to 4 servings
*Prep time: 10 minutes*
*Cook time: 25 to 30 minutes*
*Total time: 35 to 40 minutes*

This oven-roasted butternut squash with maple syrup and pecans is a simple yet brilliant combination. I've made it many times and usually pair it with a bowl of brown rice or quinoa and steamed greens. I'm grateful to my friend Ashton Ragsdale, a New York City–based food activist, wellness enthusiast, and fellow book lover, for sharing this beautiful recipe, and I hope you'll love it as much as I do.

On the inspiration for this recipe, Ashton says: "In my plant-based journey something I had been craving was the flavor maple. Maple bacon was a staple growing up in St. Louis, where meat and BBQ culture is king. And with this recipe I was able to remain connected to my roots, but with a twist. Squash isn't bacon, but I'd take this over maple bacon any day! My goal with recipes is to recreate meals from my African American lineage and turn them vegan to open people's minds to plant-based foods with flavor."

**1 butternut squash (4½ cups/475 g), either peeled or with the skin, depending on your personal preference, seeds removed, cubed**

**4 to 4½ teaspoons olive oil**

**4½ teaspoons maple syrup**

**½ teaspoon sea salt**

**1 cup (115 g) pecans**

**A few sprigs of fresh rosemary**

**1.** Preheat the oven to 350°F (180°C) and line a baking tray with parchment paper.

**2.** Mix all the ingredients in a large bowl, making sure all the butternut cubes are well coated.

**3.** Transfer to the baking tray and bake for 25 to 30 minutes, until the squash is tender when pierced with a fork.

"Rice & Gravy" by Smino

 GF

 LV

Wholesome

SIDE DISHES

# WHISKEY-GLAZED BRUSSELS SPROUTS & LEEKS

Yield: 4 servings

*Prep time: 15 minutes*
*Cook time: 20 minutes*
*Total time: 35 minutes*

These Whiskey-Glazed Brussels Sprouts and Leeks are intended for both vegetable lovers and those trying to be. They're an easy go-to option that you can add to weeknight dinners as well as enjoy on more festive occasions.

- ¼ cup (57 g) vegan butter
- 18 ounces (500 g) brussels sprouts, stems and outermost layer removed, then halved or quartered if large
- 1 large leek (white and green parts), thinly sliced; root end discarded
- ¼ cup (60 mL) apple cider vinegar
- ¼ cup (60 mL) whiskey
- ¼ cup (60 mL) coconut nectar or maple syrup
- 5 to 7 sprigs of fresh thyme
- ½ teaspoon sea salt, or to taste
- 1 pinch of ground black pepper
- 1 cup (240 mL) water

**1.** Melt the butter in a large pan over medium heat, add the brussels sprouts and leek, and sauté for 10 minutes, until they begin to soften, adding the fresh thyme halfway through.

**2.** Add all the remaining ingredients and bring to a boil, then reduce the heat to low and simmer for 10 minutes, until the veggies are tender and have absorbed all the flavors.

## NOTE
*You can use sliced carrots instead of or in addition to either of the vegetables used here.*

## SERVING SUGGESTIONS
*Serve with rice, savory pies, beans, or any other savory dish.*

"Hey Now (When I Give You All My Lovin')" by Romare

GF

TNF

LV

Wholesome

SIDE DISHES

# SPICY ROASTED CORN ON THE COB

Yield: 6 servings

Prep time: 15 minutes
Cook time: 30 minutes
Total time: 45 minutes

These are a great side dish for your game nights, BBQs, or any other fun occasion. If you want to turn these into party bites, simply slice your corn on the cob into smaller discs before preparing this recipe.

½ cup (112.5 g) vegan butter or (120 mL) olive oil

2 teaspoons garlic powder

2 teaspoons onion powder

1 teaspoon sea salt

½ teaspoon ground black pepper

1 teaspoon smoked paprika

½ teaspoon ground coriander

½ teaspoon ground cumin

¼ to ½ teaspoon cayenne pepper (optional)

1 pinch of red pepper flakes

6 raw ears of corn

½ cup (75 g) panko bread crumbs, gluten-free if desired

TO SERVE

Chopped fresh parsley

Dip of your choice

1. Preheat the oven to 400°F (200°C).

2. In a small pot, melt the butter and mix in all the spices.

3. Line a baking tray with parchment paper, add the corn, and brush the ears with the melted butter-spice mixture.

4. Dip the corn in the panko bread crumbs or sprinkle them on top.

5. Roast for 30 minutes.

6. Top with a little parsley and serve with the dip of your choice.

"Give it Up" by Lee Dorsey

GFO

TNF

LV

Wholesome

SIDE DISHES

# Best of Vegan Baking

**IN** **THIS CHAPTER, YOU'LL FIND** baked goods and other sweet treats. Some are renditions of classics like carrot cake and others include creative ways to bring out the flavors in fruits like pineapples and peaches. Knowing alternatives for eggs, milk, and butter will allow you to create desserts that taste just like their nonvegan counterparts.

I grew up with the German tradition of *Kaffee und Kuchen*, a social ritual dating back to the seventeenth century that takes place between 3:00 and 4:00 p.m. when you invite guests over, eat cake, and drink coffee together. What makes this time special is its ceremonial aspect. This is not a time to be distracted by anything else, but simply a moment to take a breath and enjoy good company and conversation. There is no need to be productive and no expectation to achieve anything. My paternal grandfather was of Danish, Swedish, and Norwegian descent, regions with a similar tradition called *hygge*. The term *hygge* derives from a sixteenth-century Norwegian term, *hugga*, which means "to comfort" or "to console" and is related to the English word *hug*. Nowadays, *hygge* has become synonymous with coziness, comfort, conviviality, and enjoying the moment. I love the idea of a mindset and practice that invites us to slow down and find joy in everyday moments. I hope that you may remember this and try to incorporate some *Kaffee und Kuchen* at 3:00 p.m. and apply a little *hygge* to your life whenever possible.

# MAPLE-ROASTED PINEAPPLE
## WITH MINT YOGURT

In collaboration with

Saqera Kokayi

Yield: 4 servings

*Prep time: 20 minutes*
*Cook time: 22 minutes*
*Total time: 42 minutes*

Saqera, who is both a close friend and one of our Best of Vegan editors (she writes our "Food History" column), was born and raised vegan in Brooklyn, New York, in the late 1980s and early 1990s. Her stories of eating tofu with veggies and drinking soy milk as the only nondairy alternative explain her current mindset when it comes to veganism. It's something she always rebelled against as a kid and had to reject in order to find her way back to in adulthood. She now loves to experiment with fruits and vegetables, combining them with different nuts, textures, and flavors. She doesn't feel the need to recreate nonvegan dishes because she has no memories linked to them from growing up. Instead, she embraces the unique and often intentionally simple combinations she comes up with in her Brooklyn kitchen and loves to share them with others. This recipe is an example of just that.

- 1 fresh pineapple, cored and cut into 1-inch (2.5 cm) sticks or discs
- ¼ cup (60 mL) fresh orange juice
- 1 pinch of sea salt
- 1 tablespoon brown sugar
- ¼ cup (60 mL) maple syrup
- ½ cup (120 mL) plain vegan yogurt, unsweetened
- ¼ cup (25 g) pistachios, chopped and toasted
- Chopped mint, for garnish

**1.** Preheat the oven to 400°F (200°C) and line a baking tray with parchment paper.

**2.** Marinate the pineapple sticks or discs in the orange juice for 10 minutes.

**3.** Place the pineapple sticks or discs on the baking tray and sprinkle with the salt and sugar.

**4.** Bake for 20 minutes, then broil for 2 minutes 2 to 3 inches (5 to 7.5 cm) from the heat source. The pineapple should start to caramelize.

**5.** Heat the maple syrup in a small pot until just hot, but not burn-your-mouth hot.

**6.** Serve the pineapple with a dollop of vegan yogurt, the hot maple syrup, toasted pistachios, and chopped mint.

"Honey"
by Erykah Badu

# MANGO COCONUT LIME & BASIL SORBET

Yield: 4 to 6 servings

*Prep time: 10 minutes*
*Freeze time: 4+ hours*
*Total time: 4+ hours for freezing plus 10 minutes*

This recipe is refreshing and creamy, ideal for a summer day, and with its simple ingredients, it can even be enjoyed for breakfast or as an appetizer. The fresh basil leaves are a perhaps unexpected but essential part of this sorbet.

1 14-ounce (400 mL) can full-fat coconut cream

4 cups (about 550 to 700 g) frozen mango chunks

¼ cup (60 mL) maple syrup

Juice of 1 lime (about 2 tablespoons)

1 cup (240 mL) fresh orange juice

1 pinch of sea salt

About 10 fresh basil leaves, or more to taste

**1.** In a high-speed blender, blend all the ingredients until very smooth, then transfer to a freezer-safe container.

**2.** Freeze for at least 4 hours.

**3.** Allow to thaw for a few minutes before serving.

 "What's the Use" by Jamie Lidell

 GF
 TNF
 LV

SWEET TREATS

# RUM PEACHES & CREAM

In collaboration with

Rōze Traore, Le Cordon Bleu–trained chef, previously at Eleven Madison Park, New York City

Yield: 2 servings

*Prep time: 20 minutes*
*Cook time: 15 minutes*
*Total time: 35 minutes*

Peaches and cream—a classic combo, but with a vegan twist, using coconut cream instead of dairy and packed with flavor from fresh vanilla bean, rum, lime, coconut flakes, and fresh mint leaves. Rōze, a friend I met through our common friend Adam Kenworthy (see page 145), is a traditionally trained nonvegan chef who enjoys a challenge and sees plant-based cuisine as something to embrace and experiment with rather than shun or dismiss. When he was just eighteen, he enrolled in Le Cordon Bleu in Paris and has since worked in some of the world's most prestigious kitchens, including Eleven Madison Park and the NoMad. Enjoy this recipe on a warm summer night with a cocktail or mocktail.

2 peaches, sliced (unpeeled)

¼ cup (60 mL) white rum

1 vanilla bean

1 lime

1 cup coconut whipped cream, such as Forager Project Whipped Cream Alternative, So Delicious Cocowhip, or homemade (see page 208)

1 pinch of sea salt, plus more for the coconut flakes

High-heat neutral vegetable oil

½ cup (30 g) coconut chips or flakes

A sprinkle of sugar

*FOR SERVING*
**Fresh mint leaves, for garnish**

1. **Prepare the peaches:** Place the peaches in a bowl. Pour the rum over them and let marinate for 10 to 15 minutes. Meanwhile, preheat a grill to 380°F (195°C). If using a grill pan and stovetop instead, you can skip this step.

2. **For the whipped cream:** Slice the vanilla bean in half and scrape the seeds out with the back of a knife. Add them to a medium bowl along with a teaspoon of lime zest and a squeeze of lime juice. Pour in the whipped cream and season with a pinch of salt.

3. Whisk for 1 to 2 minutes, until well combined. Place in the fridge while you grill the peaches.

4. **For the coconut chips:** Place a medium skillet over medium heat. Drizzle enough oil to coat the bottom of the pan, then add the coconut chips and season with salt and sugar. Cook, stirring constantly, until golden, about 7 minutes.

5. Pour a little oil on a rag and rub the grates of the grill to prevent sticking. Place the peaches on the grill (or use a grill pan over medium to high heat on your stovetop, heating it just a few minutes before adding the peaches) and cook for 3 minutes on each side, until you see grill marks.

6. Serve the peaches with the coconut cream, sprinkled with the toasted coconut, and garnished with mint leaves.

"Every Night" by Walker Lukens

GF

Best of Vegan Baking

SWEET TREATS

# BELGIAN WAFFLES
## TWO WAYS

Did you know that there are two main types of waffles in Belgium? If you've never been to this tiny country in the heart of Europe, chances are the only kind you've tried are Brussels-style waffles. The other kind, Liège-style waffles, named after the city of Liège near the Belgium-Germany border, may not be as well known in the world, but they are certainly just as popular in Belgium.

Waffles are a common snack, and they're also street food in Belgium, and you'll often find waffle shops near train and bus stations, where people grab a hot waffle on their way to or from work or during their lunch break. The main difference between the two types of waffles is that Brussels waffles are made with a batter and are thinner and softer, whereas Liège waffles are much thicker and made with a dough and folded-in pearl sugar. Traditionally, you would also use different waffle irons for each kind of waffle, but if you don't have two irons, it's absolutely fine to use the same as it won't impact the taste. I love them both, but I'll admit that I do have a slight preference for Liège waffles.

Best of Vegan Baking

**SWEET TREATS**

*CONTINUES*

# Gaufres de Bruxelles

BRUSSELS WAFFLES

1 teaspoon vanilla extract (or seeds from
½ vanilla bean)

1½ cups (360 mL) oat milk

2 cups (250 g) all-purpose flour

1 tablespoon baking powder

¼ teaspoon baking soda

¼ cup plus 2 tablespoons (75 g) fine or super fine
sugar

3 tablespoons cornstarch

⅔ cup (150 g) vegan butter, melted

1 pinch of sea salt

Confectioners' sugar

Fresh berries and vegan whipped cream,
for topping (optional)

**1.** In a small pot, mix the vanilla and milk and bring to a boil, then set aside and let cool for a few minutes.

**2.** Combine the flour, baking powder, baking soda, sugar, and cornstarch in a bowl, then add the warm milk and beat well using a whisk until you get a smooth batter and there are no lumps. Add the melted butter to the batter and whisk again.

**3.** Let the batter rest in the fridge for an hour.

**4.** Grease and heat your waffle iron. Pour the batter into the waffle iron and cook according to the iron's instructions.

**5.** Serve immediately, or keep the finished waffles warm in the oven at low heat while you cook the rest of the batter.

**6.** Sprinkle with confectioners' sugar and serve with your desired toppings.

Yield: 8 waffles

*Prep time: 15 minutes*
*Rest time: 1 hour*
*Cook time: 20 minutes*
*Total time: 1 hour, 35 minutes*

"Bruxelles Je T'aime"
by Angèle

SWEET TREATS

# Gaufres de Liège

LIÈGE WAFFLES

0.6 ounces (16 g) fresh baker's yeast (see Note)

4 tablespoons (50 g) granulated sugar

⅔ cup (160 mL) oat milk, lukewarm

½ cup (112.5 g) vegan butter, softened

2 teaspoons vanilla extract

2⅓ cups plus 1 tablespoon (300 g) all-purpose flour

¼ cup plus 3 tablespoons (105 mL) aquafaba
(the liquid from a can of chickpeas)

½ teaspoon sea salt

½ cup (75 g) Belgian pearl sugar (see Notes)

**1.** In a large bowl, mix the yeast, 2 tablespoons of the granulated sugar, and the milk using a whisk or a fork.

**2.** In a separate bowl, mix the butter with the remaining 2 tablespoons granulated sugar and the vanilla extract until well incorporated.

**3.** Add the flour, aquafaba, butter mix, and salt to the large bowl with the yeast mixture, and mix using a spatula or wooden spoon until you have a sticky dough.

**4.** Cover the bowl and let the dough rest at room temperature for 30 minutes.

**5.** Fold the pearl sugar into the dough and let rest for another 30 minutes.

**6.** Preheat and grease the waffle iron and cook according to the iron's instructions.

Yield: 8 waffles

*Prep time: 15 minutes*
*Rest time: 1 hour*
*Cook time: 20 minutes*
*Total time: 1 hour, 35 minutes*

## NOTES

• *Fresh baker's yeast is usually found as small cubes in the refrigerated section.*

• *If you can't find Belgian pearl sugar, you can make your own by adding sugar cubes to a resealable bag and then smashing them into smaller (peanut-size) pieces using a hammer or other heavy object.*

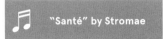
"Santé" by Stromae

SWEET TREATS

# VEGAN
# TIRAMISU

Carlo Cao, creator of Vegaliciously, chef, and cookbook author

Yield: 8 servings

*Prep time: 20 minutes*
*Cook time: 22 minutes*
*Rest time: 8 to 10 hours*
*Total time: 10 hours resting plus 42 minutes*

Tiramisu, which means "pull me up" in Italian, is a coffee-based dessert with a ladyfingers base, a creamy mascarpone filling, and a topping of cacao powder. It is undoubtedly my favorite dessert of all time. I grew up eating it, and my love for it only intensified when I lived in Italy in my late teens and early twenties.

When it comes to veganized Italian cuisine, Carlo Cao is an expert. He is a fellow vegan food blogger whose work I admire and who's been featured on Best of Vegan many times. His Italian mother and grandmother taught him how to cook and continue to inspire many of his recipes. This recipe is an adaptation of the veganized family recipe Carlo included in his cookbook *The Italian Kitchen Vegan Edition*, available as an e-book in English. With his blessing, I've made a few adjustments to make it tree-nut free.

🎵 "Sognami" by Biagio Antonacci

## FOR THE SPONGE CAKE
- 1½ cups plus 2 tablespoons (200 g) all-purpose flour
- ¾ cup (150 g) cane sugar
- 2 teaspoons baking powder
- ¼ cup (57 g) vegan butter, melted
- ¼ teaspoon sea salt
- ¾ cup (180 mL) cold sparkling water

## FOR THE COFFEE
- 1 cup (240 mL) boiling water
- 2 tablespoons instant coffee
- ½ cup (120 mL) amaretto, or more cofee with a few drops of almond extract for an alcohol-free version

## FOR THE VEGAN MASCARPONE CREAM
- 10.5 ounces (300 g) silken tofu, drained
- 1 14-ounce can (400 mL) full-fat coconut cream, solid part only
- ½ cup (100 g) superfine sugar
- 2 teaspoons vanilla extract
- 1 pinch of sea salt
- 3 tablespoons refined coconut oil, solid

## FOR TOPPING
Cacao powder

**1.** Preheat the oven to 350°F (180°C). Line a baking tray with parchment paper. The tray should be about twice the size of the tiramisu dish you'll be using.

**2. Prepare the sponge cake:** Place all the ingredients in a large bowl and mix briefly with a spatula or wooden spoon until smooth (don't overmix).

**3.** Pour the batter into the baking tray.

**4.** Bake on the middle rack of the oven for 20 to 22 minutes. While the cake is baking, prepare the coffee: Mix the boiling water and instant coffee (you can also use brewed coffee or espresso) and let it cool completely in the fridge. Once cooled, mix in the amaretto and set aside.

**5.** Remove the sponge cake from the oven and allow it to cool completely (this will take up to an hour and can be accelerated by placing the cake in the fridge), then flip the cake upside down onto a clean work surface and peel off the parchment paper.

**6.** Cut the cake into smaller strips (to resemble the traditional ladyfinger biscuits that are used) or in half. If cutting into strips, cut to approximate the size of ladyfingers.

**7. Prepare the mascarpone cream:** Add all the ingredients to a high-speed blender or food processor and blend for 1 minute, or until everything is well incorporated and you get a smooth consistency. Place in the fridge to set.

**8.** If you cut the cake in half, place one layer in a 10 x 12-inch (25 x 30 cm) glass or ceramic deep dish with the bottom side facing up (that will make it absorb the coffee more easily), then pour half of the coffee mixture onto the cake using a spoon. If you cut the cake into smaller strips, dip the strips into the coffee and then place them into the dish in a single layer.

**9.** Evenly spread the filling over the coffee-soaked sponge cake. Add another layer of cake, coffee mixture, and filling, then dust with cacao powder. Refrigerate to set for at least 8 to 10 hours before serving.

# VEGAN
# PRETZELS

In collaboration with

Katharina Arrigoni, award-winning
baker, cookbook author, and
creator of BesondersGut

Yield: 10 pretzels or breadsticks

*Prep time: 30 minutes*
*Cool time: 2 to 8 hours*
*Rest/proof time: 1 hour, 40 minutes*
*Cook time: 24 minutes*
*(12 minutes per batch)*
*Total time: 4 to 10 hours*
*plus 34 minutes*

The following two recipes are contributions by one of my biggest pastry idols, Katharina Arrigoni. Her book *Lieblingsbrote* (which means "favorite breads" in German) is visually mesmerizing, filled with the most beautiful breads for every occasion. For this book, I asked her to help me recreate a childhood favorite, pretzels. I used to love walking to the local bakery to buy classic soft pretzels, as well as *Laugenstangen* ("lye sticks," which are essentially just pretzel sticks). This recipe is a vegan twist on the classic pretzel. For a visual tutorial on how to shape the dough pockets, refer to bestofvegan .com/mycookbook. Enjoy!

## NOTE
*The following two recipes include weights (in ounces and grams) rather than volumes for most of the ingredients to ensure accuracy. You can use a kitchen or letter scale.*

FOR THE DOUGH

**8.8 ounces (250 g) cold water (about 42°F/6°C)**

**0.7 ounce (20 g) refined canola oil**

**0.3 ounce (8 g) fresh baker's yeast**

**0.21 ounce (6 g) non-diastatic malt (optional)**

**15.85 ounces (450 g) white wheat flour or all-purpose flour**

**1.75 ounces (50 g) fine whole-wheat flour**

**1½ teaspoons sea salt**

TO FINISH

**Food-grade lye (see Note) or baking soda**

**Coarse salt to taste (optional)**

**1. Prepare the dough/ first proof (start this in the morning):** Place all the dough ingredients in the bowl of a stand mixer in the order in which they are listed. Using the dough hook, knead the dough at the slowest speed for 5 to 8 minutes.

**2.** Increase the speed and continue kneading for another 5 to 8 minutes. The result should be a firm yet smooth dough. You can also knead the dough by hand, but it may take longer to reach the desired consistency.

**3.** Tightly cover the bowl with plastic wrap so it is airtight and let rest at 70°F to 73.5°F (21°C to 23°C) for 30 minutes.

**4. Form the pretzels/second proof:** Turn the dough out onto an unfloured surface and, using a dough scraper, divide it into 10 equal portions. Use a kitchen scale to ensure that the portions are about the same weight (about 2.8 ounces/80 g each).

**5.** Roll the dough pieces into balls, then form dumpling-like dough pockets, sealing them well. Cover with a damp kitchen towel and let rest for 10 minutes.

**6.** Next, use your hands to roll them into strands about 27.5 inches (70 cm) long. You want them thicker in the middle and thinner toward the ends.

**7.** Loop the strands to form the pretzels and place on two baking sheets lined with parchment papers. Cover with a dry kitchen towel and let rest for an hour at 70°F to 73.5°F (21°C to 23°C).

**8.** Uncover the pretzels and refrigerate at 39°F to 43°F (4°C to 6°C ) for 2 to 8 hours.

*CONTINUES*

**9.** Preheat the oven to 425°F (220°C).

**10.** Take 5 pretzels out of the fridge (they should be stiff and a little dried out), add the lye (see Note) or baking soda (see box at right), and place back on the parchment paper, making sure there's a little space between the pretzels.

**11.** Score the thickest part of the pretzel at a flat angle using a sharp knife. Sprinkle with coarse salt, if desired.

**12.** Bake immediately for about 12 minutes. During the first 4 minutes, open the oven door briefly once or twice.

**13.** Repeat with the second batch of pretzels.

### NOTE

*Lye is applied by dissolving 1.31 ounces (37 g) of lye powder In a bowl with 4 cups (1 L) of cold water and then dipping the pretzels into the bowl for 10 to 15 seconds each. Please follow the necessary safety precautions (like wearing protective eyewear, long sleeves, and surgical gloves) when working with food-grade lye. It's very acidic and can be dangerous.*

"1ste Liebe" by Max Herre, feat. Joy Denalane

# LYE & BAKING SODA TIPS

The exact safety precautions, and further instructions on how to use lye with pretzels can be found on the food-grade lye's package. In case you would like a more detailed step-by-step guide, we've included one on bestofvegan.com/mycookbook.

If using baking soda instead, follow these steps:

**1** Prep your baking soda by baking it (this step is optional, but will improve the end result): bake ½ cup (115 g) baking soda on a baking tray lined with aluminum foil at 250°F/120°C for 1 hour.

**2** In a large pot, bring the baked baking soda and 8 cups (2 L) water to a boil. Next, dip the pretzels in the boiling water 1 or 2 at a time for 10 to 15 seconds each. Remove using a slotted spoon.

**Note:** Baking soda is not as dangerous as lye, but it can still be irritating, so be sure to avoid skin and eye contact.

# CACAO CHALLAH

In collaboration with

Katharina Arrigoni (BesondersGut)

Yield: 1 large or 2 small challah(s)

Prep time: 1 day
Rest time: 2 hours, 40 minutes
Cook time: 45 to 50 minutes
Total time: 1 day for the starter plus
3 hours, 25 to 30 minutes

Katharina's famous vegan challah recipes are among the most popular ones we've ever shared on Best of Vegan. In biblical Hebrew, *challah* meant "loaf" or "cake." It is traditionally made with eggs, giving it a brioche-like texture, and is typically eaten on Shabbat, and for Jewish holidays and celebrations. This particular challah recipe includes a hint of chocolate thanks to the added cacao powder (often referred to as cocoa).

Plan ahead when making challah! You need to make the poolish the day before you plan to bake the bread.

## NOTE
*Just like the previous recipe, this recipe uses weight instead of volume to allow for more accuracy. And, for a visual tutorial on how to shape the dough pockets, refer to bestofvegan .com/mycookbook.*

### FOR THE STARTER/POOLISH
3.5 ounces (100 g) water

0.035 ounces (1 g) fresh yeast

3.5 ounces (100 g) white or light spelt flour

### FOR THE DOUGH
2.45 ounces (70 g) canola oil

4.6 ounces (130 g) water

0.28 ounces (8 g) fresh baker's yeast

4½ teaspoons maple syrup

12.7 ounces (360 g) white wheat flour or bread flour, plus more for dusting

1.41 ounces (40 g) cacao powder

1½ teaspoons sea salt

**1. Make the starter/poolish:** Start this the day before you plan to bake. Pour the water into a medium bowl and mix with the yeast.

**2.** Add the flour, mix, and cover with a lid or plastic wrap. Let it rest at 70°F to 73.5°F (21°C to 23°C) for 2 hours to allow the yeast to do its work.

**3.** Transfer the starter to the fridge and let rest until the next day. The starter should at least double in size.

**4. Prepare the dough/first proof:** On the next day, take the starter out of the refrigerator 1 hour before you plan to use it. Place all the dough ingredients, including the complete starter, in the bowl of a stand mixer in the order in which they are listed. Using the dough hook, knead the dough for 8 to 10 minutes at the slowest speed.

**5.** If the dough seems unusually sticky or even gooey, no need to worry! Simply gently knead for another 3 to 5 minutes until the dough is smooth and soft. You can also knead the dough by hand, but it may take a little longer to reach the desired consistency.

**6.** The ideal temperature of the dough should be: 73.5 to 77°F (23 to 25°C). Cover the bowl so it is airtight and let rest at 70 to 73.5°F (21 to 23°C) for 1 hour. (Refer to bestofvegan .com/mycookbook for more details.)

**7. Form the dough/second proof:** Turn the dough out onto an unfloured surface. Use a dough scraper to divide the dough into equal portions (the number depends on how you like to braid the challah and whether you are making one or two loaves; see Notes), then use a kitchen scale to ensure that the portions are about the same weight.

BREADS

*CONTINUES*

**8.** Roll the dough pieces into balls, then form dumpling-like dough pockets, sealing them well. Cover with a dry kitchen towel and let rest for 10 minutes.

**9.** Roll the dough balls into strands. At this point you may need a little flour, but use as little as possible so the dough does not get too dry. Dust the finished strands with just a little flour, then braid the challah(s) and place on a baking sheet lined with parchment paper (see Notes).

**10.** Cover the dough with a large bowl so it doesn't dry out and let rest for another 30 to 45 minutes.

**11. Bake the challah:** Preheat the oven to 375°F (190°C).

**12.** Dust the braid evenly with a little flour right before baking and use a sharp knife to score the strands (see photo).

**13.** Bake for 10 minutes with steam (see Notes). After 10 minutes, release some of the steam by briefly opening the oven door.

**14.** Then, bake for another 35 minutes at the same temperature. (If making two smaller challahs, reduce the final baking time to 25 to 30 minutes.)

## NOTES

• *Go to bestofvegan.com/mycookbook to view challah braiding tutorials.*

*There are two methods of adding steam to your oven:*

• *Place a large baking tray in the bottom of your oven while you preheat it. Fill the tray with boiling water (as much as possible) right after you add the challah, then quickly close the oven door. Ideally, you will hear the water sizzle as it is poured into the tray.*

• *Use a spray bottle filled with water to generously spray (4 to 5 sprays) the challah while it's already in the oven, then quickly close the oven door. (This is recommended if the bottom of your oven doesn't usually get hot enough, for instance.)*

"The River of Dreams" by Billy Joel

"[Breadmaking is] one of those almost hypnotic businesses, like a dance from some ancient ceremony. It leaves you filled with one of the world's sweetest smells . . . there is no chiropractic treatment, no Yoga exercise, no hour of meditation in a music-throbbing chapel that will leave you emptier of bad thoughts than this homely ceremony of making bread."
—M.F.K. FISHER, *The Art of Eating*

# FRISIAN-INSPIRED
# SODA BREAD
# ROLLS

In collaboration with

Rens Kroes

Yield: 6 bread rolls

*Prep time: 10 minutes*
*Cook time: 25 minutes*
*Total time: 35 minutes*

With these Frisian-inspired bread rolls, Rens and I want to honor our Frisian ancestries. Rens's family is from the town of Gytsjerk in Friesland, a northern region of the Netherlands with its own traditions and language. It's the same region my paternal grandmother's ancestors were from. In their hometown, Rens's great-grandfather Kloosterman owned a bakery by the same name, and Rens grew up learning how to make bread from scratch. Traditional Frisian rye bread, which was my father's favorite too, is a dark loaf reminiscent of pumpernickel bread that takes careful preparation and a very long time to bake at low temperatures. These bread rolls combine some of the same ingredients, like rye and apple syrup, with elements of Irish soda bread in order for it to remain yeast-free. We wanted to create a Frisian-inspired recipe that is slightly more user-friendly, requiring much less preparation and cook time. If you're interested in traditional rye bread, you can find our recipe for it at bestofvegan.com/mycookbook.

1 cup (240 mL) soy, almond (contains tree nuts), or oat milk

1 tablespoon apple cider vinegar

2⅓ cups plus 1 tablespoon (300 g) white spelt flour

½ cup (55 g) rye flour (or more spelt flour)

2 tablespoons plus 1½ teaspoons oat bran

1 teaspoon baking soda

1 teaspoon sea salt

1 tablespoon apple syrup (see Notes)

⅓ cup (50 g) raisins (optional)

1 tablespoon sunflower seeds

1 tablespoon rye flakes

⅓ cup (80 mL) water

**1.** Preheat the oven to 425°F (220°C), placing the oven rack toward the lower part of the oven. Place six small ramekins in a large Dutch oven or similar pot and line them with parchment paper (see Notes).

**2.** In a small bowl, mix the milk and apple cider vinegar and set aside to form buttermilk.

**3.** In a separate, bigger bowl, mix the flours, oat bran, baking soda, and salt, then slowly incorporate the buttermilk and apple syrup using a wooden spoon or spatula until you get a sticky dough.

**4.** Fold in the raisins (if using), then divide the dough among the lined ramekins.

**5.** Using a sharp knife, score the tops in an X shape, then top with the sunflower seeds and the rye flakes.

**6.** Pour the water in the bottom of the Dutch oven (it will touch the ramekins, but not the dough) to create steam while baking.

**7.** Cover the Dutch oven with a lid and bake for 25 minutes.

**8.** The bread rolls are best enjoyed straight out of the oven. If you consume them at a later point, be sure to reheat them a little to soften.

## NOTES

• *Apple syrup is a thick, dark spread that looks similar to molasses. It's not the kind of syrup you would add to drinks. If you can't find it, you can use date syrup instead. The sweetness helps balance out the bitterness of the baking soda.*

• *The Dutch oven with lid is needed to prevent the bread rolls' crust from getting too hard.*

 "Dûnsje Mei Dy" by Piter Wilkens

# CHOCOLATE CHIP COOKIES

Yield: 9 cookies

Prep time: 10 minutes
Cook time: 10 minutes
Cool time: 5 to 10 minutes
Total time: 25 to 30 minutes

After trying many different variations, I finally created my ideal chocolate chip cookie recipe. I personally love cookies that are thin and crisp, yet still on the chewy side. You'll see that this recipe is super easy to make and best enjoyed with a glass of ice-cold plant milk.

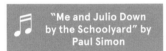
"Me and Julio Down by the Schoolyard" by Paul Simon

COOKIES

Best of Vegan Baking

- ¼ cup (57 g) vegan butter, cold and grated or cut into chunks
- ¼ cup (50 g) packed brown sugar
- ¼ cup (50 g) cane sugar
- ½ teaspoon vanilla extract
- 1 cup (125 g) all-purpose flour (see Note)
- ½ teaspoon baking soda
- 1 pinch of sea salt
- 1 tablespoon unsweetened oat milk or other plant milk
- 1.75 ounces (50 g) dark vegan chocolate, roughly chopped
- ¼ to ½ teaspoon sea salt flakes

**1.** Preheat the oven to 350°F (180°C). Position a rack slightly above the middle of the oven.

**2.** In a large bowl, cream the vegan butter, milk, and sugars using an electric mixer. (If you don't have an electric mixer, you can use a wooden spoon or your hands.)

**3.** Add all the remaining ingredients except the chopped chocolate and sea salt flakes and continue mixing for 30 seconds, until you reach a crumbly consistency. Then knead it into a dough ball using your hands (if the dough is too crumbly or dry, add ½ to 1 teaspoon of extra milk, but be careful not to add too much).

**4.** Either fold all the chocolate into the dough or fold in only half of it and set the other half aside for topping the baked cookies (I personally prefer the second option).

**5.** Form 9 cookie dough balls (using a cookie or ice cream scoop will help) and place them on a cookie sheet lined with parchment paper. (If you don't have a cookie scoop, divide the dough into 3 equal balls and then divide each of those into 3 more equal balls to get 9 total.) Leave at least 1 inch (2.5 cm) of space between the cookies, as they'll spread while baking.

**6.** Bake the cookies for 9 to 10 minutes, until they have spread and the chocolate has started to melt.

**7.** Take the cookies out of the oven and, if you set aside half of the chocolate, dot the cookies with the remaining chocolate chunks. Sprinkle the sea salt flakes on top.

**8.** Let the cookies cool for at least 10 minutes, then enjoy with a cold glass of plant milk!

## SUGGESTED ALTERATIONS
- *To turn these into double chocolate chip cookies, add 1 tablespoon cacao powder and ½ teaspoon oat milk to the dough at the same time as the flour.*
- *To switch up the chocolate chunks, add and/or replace them with any of the following: vegan white chocolate chunks, mini vegan marshmallows, or chopped vegan caramel bonbons.*

## NOTE
*For even crispier and thinner cookies, only use ¾ cup plus 2 tablespoons (110 g) flour. For the best result, I recommend weighing the flour.*

# GLUTEN-FREE
# ALMOND TAHINI COOKIES

Yield: 9 cookies

*Prep time: 5 minutes*
*Cook time: 10 minutes*
*Cool time: 5 minutes*
*Total time: 20 minutes*

With their almond base, these cookies are reminiscent of marzipan, a sugary almond paste that is often used to decorate cakes, but is also sold as little balls called "marzipan potatoes" at Christmas markets across central Europe. The tahini lends a nuttiness that works perfectly with the other ingredients. With the two different versions—almond on almond or vanilla chocolate chip—you can mix it up or even add your own favorite toppings. This recipe can easily be doubled in case nine cookies are just not enough!

1 cup (100 g) almond flour

2 tablespoons tapioca flour (see Notes)

¼ cup (60 mL) tahini (see Notes)

¼ cup (60 mL) maple syrup

1 teaspoon almond extract (for the almond on almond version)

1 teaspoon vanilla extract (for the vanilla chocolate chip version)

½ teaspoon baking soda

1 pinch of sea salt

⅓ cup (25 g) thinly sliced almonds (or almond flakes)

¼ cup (45 g) vegan chocolate chips (for the vanilla chocolate chip version)

Sea salt flakes to top (optional, but highly recommended)

**1.** Preheat the oven to 350°F (180°C) and line a baking tray with parchment paper.

**2.** In a medium bowl, mix the almond flour, tapioca flour, tahini, maple syrup, almond or vanilla extract, baking soda, and sea salt until well combined.

**3.** Fold in the sliced almonds (and chocolate chips for the vanilla chocolate chip version).

**4.** Using a small cookie scoop or a spoon, form 9 cookie dough balls and set them on the lined baking tray. Press them down gently to form the cookies. No need to separate them too much since they'll expand only a little while baking. Sprinkle a pinch of sea salt flakes on each cookie if desired.

**5.** Bake for 10 minutes, then let cool for at least 5 minutes.

## NOTES

• *You can replace the tapioca flour with cornstarch or even omit it, but don't add more almond flour to substitute.*

• *If the oil has risen to the top of your tahini jar, be sure to mix it into the tahini before using it.*

 **"You" by Lucy Pearl**

GF

LV

Best of Vegan Baking

COOKIES

185

# CARROT CARDAMOM CAKE
## WITH LEMON CREAM CHEESE FROSTING

Yield: 8 slices/1 loaf

*Prep time: 20 minutes*
*Cook time: 1 hour to 1 hour, 10 minutes*
*Total time: 1 hour, 20 to 30 minutes*

This fluffy and moist carrot cake features a hint of cardamom, crunchy hazelnuts, and a refreshing lemon cream cheese frosting.

**FOR THE CAKE**
2 tablespoons chia seeds
5 tablespoons (75 mL) water
⅔ cup (160 mL) soy milk
1 tablespoon apple cider vinegar
⅓ cup (80 mL) maple syrup
⅓ cup (40 g) coconut sugar
¼ teaspoon grated nutmeg
1 teaspoon ground cinnamon
½ teaspoon ground cardamom
2 teaspoons almond extract (or vanilla extract)
⅓ cup (80 mL) sunflower seed oil
1 cup (125 g) all-purpose flour (see Note for a gluten-free option)
1 cup (95 g) almond flour
2 teaspoons baking powder
1 teaspoon baking soda
1½ cups (100 g) grated carrots
⅓ cup (40 g) chopped hazelnuts

**FOR THE CREAM CHEESE FROSTING**
1 cup (200 g) vegan cream cheese, preferable soy- or cashew-based
3 tablespoons maple syrup
Juice and grated zest of ½ lemon (1 tablespoon juice)
1 teaspoon vanilla extract
1 pinch of ground cardamom
1 tablespoon tapioca starch (optional)

**TOPPING**
2 tablespoons chopped hazelnuts

**1.** Preheat the oven to 350°F (180°C). Grease a 9 x 5-inch (23 x 12.5 cm) loaf pan or line it with parchment paper.

**2. Make the cake:** Prepare 2 chia "eggs" by mixing the chia seeds and water in a small bowl. Set aside to thicken for 2 to 3 minutes.

**3.** In a large bowl, mix the milk and vinegar and let rest for 2 to 3 minutes until it thickens.

**4.** Add the maple syrup, sugar, nutmeg, cinnamon, cardamom, almond extract, and sunflower oil. Mix well, then add the all-purpose and almond flours, baking powder, and baking soda, and mix again.

**5.** Fold in the chia "eggs," carrots, and hazelnuts using a spatula, then transfer the cake batter to the prepared pan and bake for 1 hour to 1 hour and 10 minutes, or until a toothpick comes out clean.

**6. While the cake is baking, prepare the frosting:** Mix all the ingredients using an electric mixer. Refrigerate until the cake is ready.

**7.** Let the cake cool before spreading the frosting on top using a spatula. Sprinkle the chopped hazelnuts over the frosting.

## NOTE
*For a gluten-free version, use 2 cups (150 g) 1:1 gluten-free all-purpose flour blend (Bob's Red Mill works best) and omit both the all-purpose flour and the almond flour from the ingredients.*

"Soul Cake" by Sting and "Tempo de Amor" by Herbie Hancock and Cèu

# ROYAL VATRUSHKA CAKE

In collaboration with

Anna Kotlyarova

Yield: 1 10-inch (25 cm) cake

(serves 8 to 12)

*Prep time: 25 minutes*
*Cook time: 40 to 50 minutes*
*Cool time: Ideally, a few hours or up to*
*a day in the fridge*
*Total time: Cool time (up to a day) plus*
*1 hour, 5 minutes to 1 hour, 15 minutes*

Anna is a Best of Vegan senior editor who also frequently contributes to "Food Stories," a column dedicated to recipes that members of the Best of Vegan community grew up eating and the stories behind them. Raised in Moscow, Anna didn't realize how nostalgic she felt about Eastern European cuisine, especially desserts, until she moved to New York (where she and I met) and started traveling to many other places around the globe as well. One of these desserts is Royal Vatrushka, a yeast dough and cottage cheese cake that resembles Danishes. This recipe is Anna's veganized version.

## FOR THE CRUST/TOPPING
1 cup (200 g) sugar

2 cups (250 g) all-purpose flour

1 pinch of sea salt

1 cup (225 g) vegan butter or margarine, cold

## FOR THE FILLING
18 ounces (500 g) medium-firm tofu, drained

1 ripe banana, mashed

Juice and grated zest of 1 small lemon (2 tablespoons)

½ cup (100 g) sugar

1 tablespoon vanilla extract

1 tablespoon cornstarch

**1.** Preheat the oven to 350°F (180°C) and line a 10-inch (25 cm) springform pan with parchment paper.

**2. First, make the crust:** Mix the sugar, flour, and salt in a bowl. Grate or cut the cold butter into the dry ingredients and mix it in using a stand mixer with the dough hook attachment (or use your hands). The result should be crumbly and soft like wet sand. Place it in the fridge.

**3. Combine all the filling ingredients** and blend in a blender or food processor until homogenous. If the tofu was too firm and the mix is too dry, add a splash of plant milk.

**4.** Place two-thirds of the dry mix in the pan and press lightly against the bottom and sides. Spoon the filling on top and spread evenly. Sprinkle the remaining dry mix over the filling.

**5.** Bake for 40 to 50 minutes, or until the top is golden. While traditionally served cold, you can enjoy while still warm.

**"A Sneg Idjot"** by Maya Kristalinskaya

# MINT CHIP BAKED ALASKA

In collaboration with

Bronwyn Fraser, creator of Crumbs and Caramel

Yield: 10 servings

*Prep time: 30 minutes*
*Cook time: 35 minutes*
*Freezing time: 8 hours*
*Total time: 8 hours freezing plus 1 hour, 5 minutes*

Talk about a show-stopping dessert. Whether it's for Christmas, Hanukkah, Kwanzaa, or New Year's Eve (or really, just whenever you feel like it!), this Baked Alaska is a sure way for you to impress your guests (and yourself). Bronwyn, the Vancouver-based recipe developer behind the blog Crumbs and Caramel, made a raspberry version of this dessert a while ago that I hadn't been able to stop thinking about, so I was delighted when she graciously agreed to create a mint chip and chocolate version for this book.

## FOR THE ICE CREAM DOME
- 2 pints (1 L) vegan mint chip ice cream, nut-free if desired
- 1 pint (500 mL) vegan chocolate fudge ice cream, nut-free if desired

## FOR THE CHOCOLATE FUDGE CAKE
- Nonstick baking spray
- ½ cup (120 mL) hot coffee or espresso
- 1 ounce (28 g) good-quality vegan chocolate, chopped
- 1 cup (125 g) all-purpose flour
- 1 cup (200 g) sugar
- ½ cup (60 g) Dutch-process cocoa powder
- ¾ teaspoon baking powder
- ½ teaspoon sea salt
- ¼ teaspoon baking soda
- ½ cup (120 mL) plant milk
- ¼ cup (60 mL) neutral vegetable oil
- 2 tablespoons white or apple cider vinegar
- 2 teaspoons vanilla extract

## FOR THE MERINGUE
- 1 cup (240 mL) reduced aquafaba, chilled (see Notes)
- 1 teaspoon cream of tartar
- 2 cups (400 g) sugar
- ⅔ cup (160 mL) water
- 1 tablespoon vanilla extract
- Few drops of green vegan gel food dye (not oil based) (optional)

**1. First, prepare the ice cream dome:** Remove the mint chip ice cream from the freezer and soften for 10 minutes. While it softens, line a 2- to 3-quart bowl (make sure it has an 8-inch diameter at the top) with plastic wrap, leaving a bit of overhang to remove the ice cream later.

**2.** Scoop the softened ice cream into the prepared bowl. Quickly spread ice cream over the bottom and up the sides of the bowl, leaving the center hollow; cover and freeze for 30 minutes.

**3.** Remove the chocolate ice cream from the freezer and soften for 10 minutes. Remove the bowl with the mint chip ice cream from the freezer and fill the cavity with the chocolate ice cream. Cover with plastic wrap and freeze overnight, or up to a month. The front of the freezer is the warmest, so it's best to keep the ice cream in the back if possible.

**4. Prepare the chocolate fudge cake:** Preheat the oven to 350°F (180°C). Spray an 8-inch (20 cm) round cake pan with nonstick baking spray and line the bottom with a circle of parchment paper.

*CONTINUES*

Best of Vegan Baking

TNF

CAKES

**5.** Pour the hot coffee into a large glass measuring cup. Add the chopped chocolate and let sit for 1 minute, then stir well, ensuring all of the chocolate melts.

**6.** In a large bowl, sift the flour, sugar, cocoa powder, baking powder, salt, and baking soda. Whisk well to evenly combine.

**7.** In a medium bowl or large liquid measuring cup, whisk together the milk, oil, vinegar, and vanilla.

**8.** Pour the wet ingredients into the dry ingredients, mixing with a spoon. Stir in the coffee and melted chocolate mixture.

**9.** Pour the batter into the prepared cake pan and bake for 30 to 35 minutes or until a toothpick inserted comes out clean or with a few baked crumbs. Don't open the oven early or your cake may collapse in the middle.

**10.** Cool the cake for 10 minutes on a wire cooling rack. Gently run a sharp knife along the sides of the cake to loosen any bits that are stuck. Gently and evenly invert the pan onto the rack. Remove the pan. Once completely cooled, gently wrap in plastic and place in the freezer.

**11. Prepare the meringue:** Set up your stand-mixer bowl and balloon whisk (or a large bowl and hand-mixer beaters) by wiping them down with white vinegar to remove any fat residue. The smallest amount of fat or oil will prevent the meringue from whipping fully.

**12.** Pour the chilled, reduced aquafaba and the cream of tartar into the bowl and whisk on high for 5 to 10 minutes, or until stiff peaks form. The meringue has reached stiff peaks if it holds its shape when the whisk is turned upside down and the meringue peak remains upright.

**13.** Wipe down a clean small pot, whisk, and candy thermometer with vinegar. Pour the sugar and water into the pot, set over medium-high heat, and gently whisk just until the sugar dissolves. Do not stir afterward. Bring to a boil, then reduce the heat to a simmer, taking care not to let it boil over. Using a candy thermometer, bring the mixture to the soft-ball stage, or 240°F (116°C), 10 to 15 minutes.

**14.** Once the soft-ball stage is reached, add the vanilla extract, taking care not to get burned, as the mixture will sputter. Add in the food dye if using. With the stand mixer running, carefully and very slowly pour the hot syrup into the whipped aquafaba. If you add it too fast the meringue will deflate and you may get flicked with hot syrup. Keep whipping on high until the temperature comes down to just above room temperature. Refrigerate for 10 to 15 minutes or until cold. The meringue will keep for a couple of days in the fridge at this point. If not using it straightaway, whip it again before applying it to the ice cream dome.

**15. Assemble the Baked Alaska:**
Remove the bowl of ice cream and the cake from the freezer. Peel off the plastic and place the cake layer on top of the ice cream. Cover with plastic wrap and place back in the freezer for at least 30 minutes.

**16.** Remove the bowl from the freezer. Remove the dessert from the bowl by flipping it upside down onto a serving plate or, if serving on a cake stand that won't fit in the freezer, a cake disc.

**17.** Spread the meringue over the ice cream and cake, ensuring there are no gaps. Create peaks and crevices with the back of a spoon or an offset spatula. If you prefer to pipe the meringue on for more texture, spread a layer of meringue on the dome first to seal it, then return it to the freezer every few minutes depending on how long it takes you to pipe.

**18.** Use a kitchen torch to toast the meringue at serving time.

## NOTES

• *To get the aquafaba, strain the water from cooking chickpeas, or drain canned chickpeas and reserve the liquid (if canned, make sure there are no additives). You should have 2 cups (480 mL) aquafaba to start (you'll get about ½ cup/120 mL per 14-ounce/400 g can, so you'd need about 4 cans). Simmer until reduced by half (you need 1 cup/240 mL; chill before using).*

• *You can make this dessert in advance and store some elements frozen. Tightly wrapped, the ice cream dome and cake will keep well in the freezer for a month or so. The meringue can also be applied to the ice cream dome and then frozen, but it will last only a couple of days in the freezer (depending on what else you have in there) until it starts absorbing freezer odor. It's not possible to wrap the meringue without damaging it.*

"I Can't Hide" by Priscilla Ahn

CAKES

# LAVENDER DONUTS

In collaboration with

Khloe Hines, head baker and
founder of Hungry Bunny Vegan
Bakery

Yield: 18 small or 12 regular donuts

*Prep time: 20 minutes*
*Cook time: 12 minutes*
*Cool time: 18 to 25 minutes*
*Total time: 50 to 57 minutes*

We first featured Khloe Hines and her vegan online bakery, which she launched in early 2020, as part of an article on bestofvegan.com highlighting female-owned vegan bakeries that ship nationwide. I've been a fan of her and her work ever since I had a chance to try her baked goods and therefore asked her to collaborate on this recipe.

Khloe's treats are fully vegan and can be shipped nationwide within the United States. If you're not in the US, this is your chance to enjoy one of her delicious donuts right at home.

## FOR THE DONUTS
Nonstick baking spray

1 cup (240 mL) plant milk

2 tablespoons vanilla extract

¼ cup (57 g) vegan butter, melted

1 tablespoon maple syrup

1 cup (200 g) raw turbinado sugar or organic cane sugar

1 teaspoon baking soda

1½ teaspoons baking powder

1 teaspoon ground cinnamon, or more to taste

¼ teaspoon grated nutmeg

¼ teaspoon sea salt

2 ⅓ cups plus 1 tablespoon (300 g) all-purpose flour (gluten-free if desired)

## FOR THE ICING
2 cups (240 g) confectioners' sugar

1 tablespoon plant milk

3 to 4 tablespoons vegan butter, softened

¼ teaspoon lavender extract

Purple food coloring (optional)

1. Preheat the oven to 350°F (180°C) and grease a donut pan with nonstick baking spray.

2. In a large bowl, combine the milk, vanilla, vegan butter, maple syrup, and sugar; whisk together.

3. Add the baking soda, baking powder, cinnamon, nutmeg, and salt and whisk until blended.

4. Add the flour and whisk until smooth.

5. Pour or spoon the batter into the donut pan, filling each cavity a little more than halfway.

6. Bake the donuts for 12 minutes, until a toothpick comes out clean, then remove from the oven and set aside to cool for 8 to 10 minutes.

7. Meanwhile, combine all the icing ingredients in a bowl and whisk or blend together until smooth.

8. Place the donuts on a cooling rack with parchment paper underneath it to catch the falling icing.

9. Working with one donut at a time, dip the top of the donut directly into the lavender icing, then place it back on the rack to allow the icing to set. Repeat with the remaining donuts, and let the icing set for 10 to 15 minutes.

 "Midnight Special" by Jimmy Smith

GFO

INF

Best of Vegan Baking

SMALLER SWEET BAKED GOODS

# CHICKPEA
# CHOCOLATE
# CHIP
# BLONDIES

In collaboration with

Katie Higgins, cookbook author and creator of Chocolate Covered Katie

Yield: 6 to 8 blondies

*Prep time: 10 minutes*
*Cook time: 30 minutes*
*Total time: 40 minutes*

When I first went vegan, there were only a few vegan blogs. One of them was Chocolate Covered Katie, dedicated to veganizing desserts with a healthy twist. She taught me that you could use cooked beans instead of flour in baked goods, among many other helpful tricks. Katie and I have since become good friends and with this recipe, we wanted to pay tribute to those famous beans. We hope you'll enjoy this treat.

- 1½ cups (1 14-ounce/400 g can) cooked chickpeas or white beans, rinsed and drained
- ¼ cup (60 mL) vegan Greek yogurt (or plain non-dairy yogurt)
- ¼ cup (60 mL) maple syrup
- ½ cup (62.5 g) all-purpose flour, gluten-free all-purpose flour, or oat flour
- ¼ cup (57 g) vegan butter, melted, then cooled
- ½ cup (100 g) light brown sugar
- 1 teaspoon baking powder
- ¼ teaspoon baking soda
- ¼ teaspoon sea salt
- ½ cup (85 g) vegan chocolate chips

**1.** Preheat the oven to 350°F (180°C). Grease or line an 8 x 8-inch (20 x 20 cm) brownie pan/baking dish with parchment paper.

**2.** Combine all the ingredients except the chocolate chips in a food processor or blender and mix until smooth.

**3.** Fold the chocolate chips into the batter, then pour the batter into the pan.

**4.** Bake for 30 minutes, until a toothpick comes out clean. Let cool before slicing. Best served warm.

"Better Git It in Your Soul" by Charles Mingus

# TEA-GLAZED
# SCONES

In collaboration with

Quentin Vennie, founder of
The Equitea Co., a Black-owned,
wellness-centered, and
impact-driven organic full-leaf
tea-blend company

Yield: 8 scones

Prep time: 25 minutes
Cook time: 20 minutes
Cool time: 20 minutes
Total time: 1 hour, 5 minutes

Quentin, a celebrated wellness expert, motivational speaker, and bestselling author from Baltimore, is the cofounder of the organic tea company Equitea, which he started after a journey of healing and years spent fighting depression, anxiety, and addiction. His teas, especially the green tea and chai, are what taught me to truly embrace loose-leaf tea, now a fierce competitor to my beloved coffee. We decided to collaborate on this recipe to showcase what the balance between having a sweet tooth and enjoying refreshing herbal tea as a wellness and self-care practice can look like.

"Tea is medicine to me, but not necessarily in the traditional sense," Quentin told me. "It nourishes my mind, my body, and my spirit. In a world full of deadlines, instant gratification, and the idea that success means overworking, tea gives me permission to slow down, to come back to myself, and to just be human—even if only for a moment."

## FOR THE SCONES

½ cup (120 mL) soy milk

1 tablespoon apple cider vinegar

1 tablespoon chia seeds

2 cups (250 g) all-purpose flour, plus more for dusting

1 tablespoon baking powder

¼ teaspoon sea salt

½ cup (100 g) superfine sugar

½ cup (112.5 g) frozen vegan butter, grated or cut into very small chunks

1 tablespoon vanilla extract

½ cup (85 g) vegan chocolate chips or 1 cup (150 g) fresh blueberries (optional)

## FOR THE GLAZE

1 cup (120 g) confectioners' sugar

2 tablespoons plus 1½ teaspoons prepared and chilled herbal tea (such as Equitea's chai mix or green tea)

**1.** Preheat the oven to 375°F (190°C).

**2.** In a bowl, mix the milk, cider vinegar, and chia seeds and set aside to thicken and form buttermilk.

**3.** In a separate large bowl, combine the flour, baking powder, salt, sugar, and butter using a pastry blender, forks, or the pulse function of your food processor. Mix the vanilla into the chia buttermilk and incorporate it all into the dough until everything is combined (don't overmix). Gently fold in the chocolate chips or blueberries, if using.

**4.** Transfer the dough to a work surface (add a little flour if it's too sticky) and instead of kneading it, gently roll it out, then fold and roll it out again two or three more times.

**5.** Place the dough on parchment paper on top of a clean work surface, then roll it into a disc approximately 8 inches (20 cm) in diameter. Transfer the dough and parchment to a baking sheet, and, using a sharp knife, cut the disc into 8 equal triangular scones.

**6.** Separate the scones slightly, then bake for about 22 to 24 minutes (start checking at 20 minutes; they should be light golden).

**7.** Let the scones cool on a wire rack while you prepare the glaze.

**8.** Using an immersion blender and a tall metal or plastic container, mix the confectioners' sugar and tea.

**9.** Spread the glaze on the cooled scones using a pastry brush or icing spatula. Let the glaze set before serving.

 "Shout Out Loud" by Amos Lee

# MINI BERLINER PFANNKUCHEN

## (Jelly-Filled Donuts)

In collaboration with

Holly Jade, creator of The Little Blog of Vegan and author of *The Little Book of Vegan Bakes*

Yield: approximately 15 to 20 donuts

*Prep time: 30 minutes*
*Proof time: 3 to 4 hours*
*Cooking time: 30 minutes*
*Total time: 4 to 5 hours*

On June 26, 1963, John F. Kennedy famously gave a speech in West Berlin where, in German, he declared, "*Ich bin ein Berliner!*" not realizing that he had just called himself a jelly-filled donut. *Berliner* is the term used to refer to a donut that is filled with jam, usually strawberry or plum, and topped with powdered sugar. It's called a Berliner only outside the city of Berlin. Berlin locals refer to it only as *Pfannkuchen*, meaning pancake. You can thus immediately tell if someone is not from Berlin by the way they order this baked good in a Berlin bakery.

I adored these as a kid and had been dreaming of a vegan version for the longest time. There was only one person I wanted to ask to veganize it—Holly Jade from The Little Blog of Vegan. She is a master of her craft and has a gift for creating the most extraordinary vegan baked goods. If you're looking for an amazing vegan baking book, be sure to check out *The Little Book of Vegan Bakes*.

Tip: These are best enjoyed the day they are made.

"Born & Raised" by Joy Denalane

- 1⅓ cup plus 2 teaspoons (330 mL) warm plant milk (about 100°F/38°C)
- 4½ teaspoons (14 g) instant dry yeast
- ¼ cup plus 2 tablespoons (75 g) superfine sugar
- 4 ¾ cups plus 1 tablespoon (600 g) self-rising flour
- ¼ teaspoon sea salt
- ¼ cup plus 2 tablespoons (100 g) vegan butter, melted
- 2 tablespoons powdered egg replacer (the equivalent of 2 eggs)
- High-heat neutral vegetable oil, for frying
- Confectioners' sugar
- Strawberry or plum jam

**1.** Place the warm milk in a bowl and sprinkle the yeast and sugar over it. Stir to combine, cover with a tea towel, and put in a warm place for 10 to 15 minutes, until frothy.

**2.** In the bowl of a stand mixer with the dough hook attachment or a separate large bowl, combine the flour and salt and stir.

**3.** In a small bowl, combine the melted vegan butter and egg substitute and stir to blend.

**4.** Add the yeast mixture and the egg mixture to the dry mixture and stir.

**5.** Knead on medium speed until smooth. This will take about 6 minutes in a mixer or 8 minutes by hand.

**6.** Transfer the dough to a lightly oiled bowl, cover with a tea towel, place in a warm area, and allow to proof for 2 to 3 hours, until doubled in size.

**7.** Turn the dough out onto a floured surface and roll it out to about a ½-inch (1.25 cm) thickness. Using a cookie cutter, cut out circles and place them on a lined baking tray.

**8.** Cover the donuts with a tea towel and place back in a warm area for about 1 hour, until doubled in size.

**9.** Fill a deep pan (you can use a deep-fat fryer) half to three-quarters full of oil and heat to 350°F (180°C).

**10.** Once the donuts have risen, gently lower them into the hot oil in batches of 3 to 4 and fry for 2 to 3 minutes on each side, or until puffed and golden brown. Using a slotted spoon, carefully take them out of the hot oil and place them on paper towels to drain.

**11.** While they are still warm, sprinkle the donuts with confectioners' sugar. Allow them to cool before filling.

**12.** Place berry jam in a piping bag and snip off the tip. Poke a hole in the side of each donut and fill.

# CHOCOLATE RASPBERRY MUFFINS

Yield: 9 large or 12 small muffins

*Prep time: 15 minutes*
*Cook time: 30 to 35 minutes*
*Total time: 40 to 50 minutes*

These muffins are incredibly rich and contain just the right mix of chocolate and fruit. They're sweet enough to qualify as cupcakes too, so feel free to add your favorite frosting and decorate them to your liking.

1½ to 2 cups (187.5 to 250 g) frozen raspberries (blueberries or pitted sweet cherries work too)

1¼ cups (250 g) superfine sugar

½ cup (120 mL) neutral vegetable oil (such as sunflower seed oil)

1 cup (240 mL) plain full-fat vegan yogurt

1 tablespoon vanilla extract

2 cups (250 g) all-purpose flour

⅓ cup (35 g) cacao powder

1 pinch of sea salt

1 teaspoon baking powder

1 teaspoon baking soda

½ cup (85 g) vegan dark chocolate chips

**1.** If using frozen raspberries, remove them from the freezer before starting the recipe to allow them to thaw for a few minutes. Then, preheat the oven to 350°F (180°C) and grease a muffin pan or line it with paper muffin cups.

**2.** In a large bowl, mix the sugar, oil, yogurt, and vanilla. Add the flour, cacao powder, salt, baking powder, and baking soda using a spatula or wooden spoon, until you get a smooth batter.

**3.** Gently fold in the chocolate chips and raspberries.

**4.** Spoon the batter into the muffin cups and bake for 30 minutes, if you're making 12 small muffins, or 35 minutes if you're making 9 larger muffins, until a toothpick comes out clean.

## VEGAN BAKING TIP

*There are many different egg replacers; the best one will depend on the specific recipe and your personal preference. For this recipe, I chose to use full-fat vegan yogurt to replace both eggs and milk. I find that it gives the muffins a moister texture and holds everything together well. For other recipes, like cookies, it's preferable to use a ground-seed egg replacer or a store-bought mung bean-based liquid egg replacer. If you're new to vegan baking and confused by all the options, I recommend following recipes from blogs or cookbooks (like this one) in the beginning. Over time, you'll get an intuitive feel for which option to use.*

 **"Sweet Pea" by Amos Lee**

# Best of Vegan Basics

**NOTE** THE FOLLOWING RECIPES are for staple foods that you can mostly find in stores, but it's always good to know how to make them just in case!

# NUT MILKS

Yield: 3½ cups (840 mL)

*Soaking time: 6 to 8 hours*
*Prep time: 10 minutes*
*Total time: 6 to 8 hours plus 10 minutes*

**1 cup nuts (about 150 g, depending on the kind of nut used) (see Notes)**

**3 cups (720 mL) water**

**1 pinch of sea salt**

*OPTIONAL ADD-INS*
**1 teaspoon maple syrup**

**½ teaspoon vanilla extract**

**1 tablespoon cacao powder (for chocolate milk)**

**1.** Soak the nuts in water to cover for at least 6 hours. Drain.

**2.** Place the drained nuts, water, and salt in a high-speed blender and blend until smooth.

**3.** Using a nut-milk bag or cheesecloth, filter the nut milk into a glass jar, squeezing out all the liquid. (see Notes)

**4.** Stir or blend in any desired add-ins. Store in the fridge and consume within a few days.

## NOTES
• *This works with many different types of nuts and even seeds, but some of the best are cashews, almonds, walnuts, hazelnuts, peanuts, macadamias, and Brazil nuts. Impatient? For an instant plant milk, simply blend ⅓ cup (80 mL) nut or seed butter with 3 cups (720 mL) water and your desired add-ins.*

• *You can keep the pulp in the freezer and use it in cookie or muffin recipes, replacing part of the flour you would normally use.*

# WALNUT PARMESAN

Yield: ¾ cup (about 145 g)

*Prep time: 5 minutes*
*Total time: 5 minutes*

**1 cup (115 g) raw unsalted walnuts (or cashews)**

**¼ cup (15 g) nutritional yeast**

**½ teaspoon sea salt**

**½ teaspoon onion powder**

**1 teaspoon garlic powder**

Mix all the ingredients in a blender or food processor (see Note) until you get a floury consistency, similar to grated parmesan. Store in an airtight container in the fridge for up to a few weeks.

## NOTE
*Make sure the blender or food processor is totally dry before adding the ingredients.*

## SERVING SUGGESTIONS
*Sprinkle on top of pasta, salads, stews, or soups.*

# ALMOND RICOTTA

<u>Yield: 1¼ cups (300 mL)</u>

*Prep time: 15 minutes*
*Cook time: 5 minutes*
*Total time: 20 minutes*

1 cup (140 g) blanched almonds
¼ cup plus 2 tablespoons (90 mL) water
Juice of 1 lemon (2 tablespoons)
1 tablespoon apple cider vinegar
1 tablespoon nutritional yeast
1 garlic clove
½ teaspoon sea salt

**1.** Boil the almonds in a pot of water for 5 minutes, then rinse with cold water and drain.

**2.** Place all the ingredients in a blender or food processor and blend until the consistency is smooth yet still a little grainy.

**3.** Store in an airtight container in the fridge and consume within 5 days.

# MOZZARELLA-STYLE PIZZA CHEESE

<u>Yield: About 1½ cups (360 mL)</u>

*Prep time: 5 minutes*
*Cook time: 10 minutes*
*Total time: 15 minutes*

½ cup (70 g) unsalted cashews
1½ cups (360 mL) water
Juice of ½ lemon (1 tablespoon)
1 teaspoon apple cider vinegar
½ teaspoon sea salt, or more to taste
1 tablespoon nutritional yeast
¼ cup (60 g) tapioca flour

**1.** Boil the cashews in a pot of water over high heat for 5 minutes, then drain.

**2.** In a high-speed blender, combine the drained cashews, ½ cup (120 mL) of the water, and the remaining ingredients (see Note). Blend on high until smooth, then add the remaining 1 cup (240 mL) water and blend again.

**3.** Transfer everything to a pot (the mixture should be quite liquid and runny).

**4.** Bring to a boil over medium to high heat while whisking constantly (this should take 1½ to 2 minutes). As soon as bubbles start forming, reduce the heat to low and cook for another 3 minutes, still whisking constantly. The cheese will thicken and become stretchy like mozzarella.

**5.** Remove from the heat and let cool or use immediately (recommended). If not being used right away, the cheese can be stored in the fridge for a few days.

## NOTE
*This recipe intentionally doesn't use many spices so that the taste remains neutral, but you can add garlic and onion powder, smoked paprika, liquid smoke, or any other condiments you'd like. (Add seasonings to the blender.)*

DAIRY ALTERNATIVES & CONDIMENTS

## SILKEN TOFU–BASED
# SOUR CREAM

Yield: 1½ cups (360 mL)

*Prep time: 10 minutes*
*Total time: 10 minutes*

10.5 ounces (300 g) silken tofu

1½ teaspoons apple cider vinegar

Juice of ½ lemon (1 tablespoon)

¼ teaspoon sea salt

Blend all ingredients in a high-speed blender until smooth. Store in the fridge for up to 3 days.

## CASHEW-BASED
# SOUR CREAM

Yield: 1 cup (240 mL)

*Prep time: 10 minutes*
*Soak time: 6 to 8 hours*
*Total time: Overnight plus 10 minutes*

1 cup (140 g) cashews

½ cup (120 mL) unsweetened plain vegan yogurt

2 tablespoons water

1½ teaspoons apple cider vinegar

Juice of ½ lemon (1 tablespoon)

¼ teaspoon sea salt

**1.** Cover the cashews with water to cover and soak for at least 6 hours. Drain, discarding the soaking water.

**2.** Blend all the ingredients in a high-speed blender until smooth. Store in the fridge for up to 3 days.

## COCONUT
# WHIPPED CREAM

Yield: 1 cup (240 mL)

*Prep time: 10 minutes*
*Total time: 10 minutes*

1 14-ounce (400 g) can full-fat coconut milk or cream, chilled

2 tablespoons confectioners' sugar, or maple syrup (or more to taste)

½ teaspoon vanilla extract (optional)

**1.** Use only the solid cream from the can—drain the liquid and discard or save for another use. Use an electric mixer to whip the coconut cream until you get a smooth consistency.

**2.** When the vegan cream is almost fully whipped, add in your sweetener of choice, and vanilla (if using) and mix again. Vegan whipped cream is best consumed right away.

## AQUAFABA
# WHIPPED CREAM

Yield: 10 servings

*Prep time: 15 minutes*
*Total time: 15 minutes*

The liquid from a 14-ounce (400 g) can of chickpeas, ideally unsalted, about ½ cup

½ cup (60 g) confectioners' sugar, or more depending on desired sweetness

½ teaspoon vanilla extract (optional)

1. Use an electric mixer to whip the aquafaba until you get a smooth and fluffy consistency. This will take at least 6 to 8 minutes.

2. When the vegan cream is fully whipped (when you turn over the bowl, it should be stiff and not fall out), add in the sugar and vanilla (if using) and mix for another 1 to 2 minutes. Enjoy right away!

# SHIITAKE BACON

Yield: ¾ cups (about 100 g)
*Prep time: 5 minutes*
*Cook time: 30 to 35 minutes*
*Total time: 35 to 40 minutes*

9 ounces (250 g) shiitake mushrooms, thinly sliced, stems discarded (about 2½ cups)

2 tablespoons olive oil

½ teaspoon smoked salt

1 pinch of smoked paprika

1 teaspoon maple syrup

1 teaspoon tamari or soy sauce

1. Preheat the oven to 350°F (180°C) and line a baking tray with parchment paper.

2. In a bowl, mix the mushrooms and oil. When the oil is well distributed, add the remaining ingredients and mix again.

3. Spread the mushrooms out on the baking tray and bake for 30 to 35 minutes, until crispy. If you're not enjoying them right away, store in an airtight container in the fridge and consume within 3 days.

# COCONUT BACON

Yield: ¾ cup (about 50 g)
*Prep time: 5 minutes*
*Cook time: 10 minutes*
*Total time: 15 minutes*

1 teaspoon liquid smoke

1 teaspoon maple syrup

1 teaspoon gluten-free tamari or soy sauce

¼ teaspoon smoked paprika

1 pinch of sea salt

¾ cup (45 g) unsweetened coconut chips (not shreds!)

1. Preheat the oven to 300°F (150°C). Line a baking tray with parchment paper.

2. Mix all the ingredients in a bowl, then spread out the flakes on the baking tray in a single layer.

3. Bake for 10 minutes, then let cool. Store in an airtight container in the fridge for up to a week.

## SERVING SUGGESTIONS
*Use in burritos or veggie bowls, with pasta, on pizza, or as a garnish for soup.*

# PUMPKIN SPICE MIX

Yield: scant ½ cup (45 g)

*Prep time: 5 minutes*
*Total time: 5 minutes*

**¼ cup (33 g) ground cinnamon**

**1 tablespoon ground ginger**

**1 tablespoon grated nutmeg**

**1½ teaspoons ground cloves**

Mix all the ingredients and store in an airtight container in the refrigerator.

## NOTE
*Nuts and seeds are best stored in the fridge as they easily become rancid at room temperature.*

## SERVING SUGGESTIONS
*Use in a pumpkin spice latte, oatmeal, granola or cereal, or pancakes.*

# EVERYTHING BUT THE BAGEL SEASONING

Yield: a little under ¾ cup (about 110 g)

*Prep time: 5 minutes*
*Total time: 5 minutes*

**3 tablespoons white sesame seeds**

**1½ teaspoons sea salt flakes**

**2 tablespoons dried minced garlic**

**2 tablespoons dried minced onion or shallots**

**4½ teaspoons black sesame seeds**

**2 tablespoons poppy seeds**

Mix all the ingredients. Store in an airtight container in the fridge or at room temperature.

## SERVING SUGGESTIONS
*Use in salads, on avocado toast, or as a crust for tofu.*

# OLIVE OIL & GARLIC HERB CUBES

*Prep time: 5 to 10 minutes (depending on how many ice cube trays you're using)*
*Total time: 5 to 10 minutes*

These cubes are a great way to reduce food waste. You can use them to sauté vegetables, make stews, soups, stir-fries, and so on.

**Fresh herbs (1 to 2 teaspoons per cube) (see Note)**
**Garlic (½ to 1 clove, minced, per cube)**
**Olive oil, as needed**

**1.** Wash the herbs and pat them dry, then chop them finely. (If you have a lot of herbs, you can also blend them.) Distribute the herbs among as many ice cube trays as needed.

**2.** Add the minced garlic to the ice cube trays with the herbs.

**3.** Fill the trays with olive oil and freeze for at least a few hours.

## NOTES
• *Herbs that freeze well this way include parsley, basil, cilantro, mint, sage, and dill.*

• *The cubes will last for 6 months.*

# COCONUT CUBES

*Prep time: 5 minutes*
*Total time: 5 minutes*

This is more of a low-waste tip than an actual recipe, but it can be very useful if you're used to cooking smaller portions and/or just want to reduce food waste and save money.

**Leftover canned coconut milk or cream**

**1.** Whisk or blend the leftover canned coconut milk or cream to ensure you have an even consistency, then pour it into ice cube trays (as many as needed), then place the tray(s) in the freezer and freeze for at least 6 to 8 hours.

**2.** You can now add cubes to your sauces, curries, stews, and soups. Simply add them to your pot while cooking and stir until fully melted.

# Acknowledgments

To the HarperCollins team, thank you for this incredible opportunity and such amazing teamwork every step of the way. A very special thank-you to Lisa Sharkey and Maddie Pillari. Lisa, thank you for helping me realize the vision for this book, for giving me so many new ideas along the way, and always saying "let's do it" to each of my ideas, no matter how unconventional. I so appreciate your enthusiasm, kindness, and encouragement. To Maddie, who edited this book, thank you for making this such a fun experience and for all your support. I, quite literally, could not have done this without you. To Sarah Weaver, the copyeditor, I am so grateful for (and impressed by) all the work you put into this book.

To my agent, Charlie Brotherstone, thank you for believing in me for all these years and for being the most empathetic, patient, and overall wonderful person. There's no one I'd rather work with.

To Laura Palese, the designer of this book. You were my first and only choice, so I'm incredibly thrilled to be working with you again. Thank you.

To my grandmother Maggie Masson and my great-uncle Johnnie Masson, thank you for teaching me your mother's recipes and spending so much time telling me all your stories, cooking the best food, and laughing together. I'm so honored to be your granddaughter and great-niece. To my mother, Martine Hendrickx, thank you for testing my recipes and being even more excited about my projects than I am. But most importantly, thank you for instilling in me my love for cooking, and the ability to always look at life a little differently. To my brother John Hansen, who inspired the "I Don't Want Salad" section of this book, thank you for humbling me and for never sugarcoating your feedback. You've always been my greatest teacher.

To the friends who've been a part of and have supported the creation of this book since day one and who are always there for me, no matter what: Jess, Sam B., Joanne, Yamina, Ko, Gena, Aurélie, Rens, and Chris. I'll forever be grateful for having you in my life.

To the contributors who were so gracious to collaborate with me and make this book as special as it is (in order of appearance): Charly and the whole Charly's Vegan Tacos team, Nkoyo Adakama, Craig Cochran, Henry Firth and Ian Theasby, WoonHeng Chia, Christine Wong, Gaz Oakley, Kayatou "Kady" Konaté, Samantha Onyemenam, Gabriel Ocasio-Cortez, Fernanda Feher and Luisa Possas, Aiescha Darmal, Yamina El Atlassi, Iromi Goonasekera Poloni, Nisha Vora, Ko Oyakawa, Kyoko Oyakawa and Miko Oyakawa, Daniel Haimona and Tracey Tawhiao, Marissa Wong, Nina Herrera, Neto, Eleni McMullin, Joanne Lee Molinaro, Samantha Bailey, Lloyd Rose, Seiran Sinjari, Sarah Kermalli, Julia Kravets, Adam Kenworthy, Gena Hamshaw, Max La Manna, Ashton Ragsdale, Saqera Kokayi, Rōze Traore, Carlo

Cao, Katharina Arrigoni, Rens Kroes, Anna Kotlyarova, Bronwyn Fraser, Khloe Hines, Katie Higgins, Quentin Vennie, and Holly Jade. Thank you all from the bottom of my heart. I knew from the beginning that there could be no Best of Vegan cookbook without the participation of some of the people I admire most. These collaborations were my favorite part of working on this book. Thank you.

A heartfelt thank-you to Marissa for helping me with part of the photography. I love what you've created, and I am so grateful for your help and your friendship. You're such a joy to work with. And thank you also to your honorary photography assistants and unofficial recipe testers, Daniel and Marley Ringkamp.

Thank you also to Seiran, Katharina, Bronwyn, and WoonHeng, who photographed their respective recipes. I love all the pictures and am honored to have them included in the book.

To the amazing recipe testers whose help I appreciate so much more than you know:

Filip V., the OG tester who's tested more recipes than anyone: You're the best, and I cannot thank you enough. To my neighbor Tjhoi Ng Sauw, who was my in-person recipe tester, thank you for always being so enthusiastic about trying all the vegan recipes. A special thank-you to Birgit Eichberger, Rosa Kurz, Amber Blicharz, Bonnie Primm, Lauren Bendik, Olivia Moffitt, Mandi Drohman, and Ilone Inge, who went above and beyond. You're amazing and I'm so grateful for your help. Thank you also to Rixlie Fozilova, Radhika Wad, Jessica Almeida, Katrin Overhage, Diana Reyes, Chrystal Caban, Micah J., Whitney Foster, Laura Tsampas, Maruta Rampane, Nomi Kane, Christine Leung, Anna Goodman, Nicole McNeely, Joy Chahal, Briana Foggin, Leslie Reitz, Sherry Lynn Fazio, Linda Timmas, and Jenna T, for being the best group of recipe testers I could have wished for. I appreciate each and every one of you.

Thank you to the contributors who provided songs from their cultures for the playlist that accompanies this book, and to my friends Sam Bailey, Jelani Day, and Adam Kenworthy for helping me curate the rest of the playlist.

Thank you also to Danny, Amos, and Priscilla. It's such an honor to have some of your beautiful songs included in this book. I know that the readers will love cooking and eating to them as much as I have.

Last but not least, most of the ceramics you'll see throughout this book were purchased from small, independent, women-owned ceramics studios whose work I simply adore. Thank you to Atelier Gilbert, Spots & Speckles, Studio Starke, and DeWe Ceramics for creating such beautiful pieces. And thank you to GreenPan for saving the day and sending me all the pans to cook in and photograph after my move across the pond.

# Playlist Recap

For extended playlists for each recipe, go to bestofvegan.com/playlist by scanning this QR code

PLAYLIST RECAP

# Bonus Content

Don't forget to e-mail your receipt or order confirmation to cookbook@bestofvegan.com to receive these bonus e-books/guides:

- Vegan Meal Prep Guide
- Vegan on a Budget
- Vegan Guide to Protein
- 7-Day Sample Meal Plan and Grocery Shopping List

## Want more vegan recipe ideas?

Many new vegans struggle with finding meal ideas because they're not yet used to what vegans eat. There are only so many recipes that fit into a cookbook, and you can find thousands of additional ones on bestofvegan.com.

Go to bestofvegan.com /mycookbook for more resources and interactive content related to this book.

# Resources

You can find an extended list of resources and an up-to-date list of recommended blogs and cookbooks on bestofvegan.com/mycookbook.

## Books

*Ageless Vegan* by Tracye McQuirter

*Eating Animals* by Jonathan Safran Foer

*How to Live Vegan* by Henry Firth and Ian Theasby

*Sistah Vegan: Food, Identity, Health, and Society: Black Female Vegans Speak* by A. Breeze Harper (editor)

*Slaughterhouse: The Shocking Story of Greed, Neglect, and Inhumane Treatment Inside the U.S. Meat Industry* by Gail Eisnitz

*Vegan for Her: The Woman's Guide to Being Healthy and Fit on a Plant-Based Diet* by Virginia Messina and JL Fields

*Vegan for Life: Everything You Need to Know to Be Healthy and Fit on a Plant-Based Diet* by Jack Norris and Virginia Messina

*Vegan Reset* by Kim-Julie Hansen

*We Are the Weather* by Jonathan Safran Foer

## Documentaries

*Earthlings:* A closer look at the conditions in which animals that are raised for food and used for other purposes live. Warning: It includes a lot of sensitive footage.

*The Game Changers:* An exploration of the link between plant-based nutrition and athletic performance and recovery.

*The Invisible Vegan:* An insight into food and identity, as well as plant-based health and wellness possibilities and practices within the African-American community.

*They're Trying to Kill Us: Diet, Poverty and Racism:* An examination of food justice and the link between nutrition, poverty, and systemic inequality.

*Vegucated:* The journey of three meat-eaters who volunteer to participate in a vegan experiment and the challenges they face.

## Websites

bestofvegan.com

carnism.org

mercyforanimals.org

nutritionfacts.org

peta.org

sanctuaries.org

thefullhelping.com

theveganrd.com

vegan.com

veganhealth.org

veganreset.com

vegansociety.com

# Index

INDEX

# About the Author

**KIM-JULIE HANSEN** is the food writer and photographer behind the Best of Vegan and Vegan Reset brands, as well as the author of *Vegan Reset: The 28-Day Plan to Kickstart Your Healthy Lifestyle* (known as *The 28-Day Vegan Plan* in the UK). She is based in both Brooklyn, New York, and Ostend, Belgium, and loves to share all things veganism and plant-based living with her audience of over two million people online. She is also a passionate advocate for social justice and mental health.